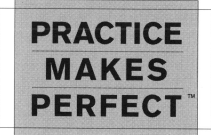

MASTERING

Vocabulary

PRACTICE MAKES PERFECT™

MASTERING
Vocabulary

Gary Robert Muschla

New York Chicago San Francisco Lisbon London Madrid Mexico City
Milan New Delhi San Juan Seoul Singapore Sydney Toronto

1 2 3 4 5 6 7 8 9 10 11 12 13 14 15 16   QDB/QDB   1 9 8 7 6 5 4 3 2

ISBN   978-0-07-177277-8
MHID   0-07-177277-4

e-ISBN   978-0-07-177759-9
e-MHID   0-07-177759-8

Library of Congress Control Number 2012931070

For Judy and Erin, as always.

Contents

About This Book   xiii

How to Use This Book   xv

Lesson 1   Synonyms, I **1**
1.1   A Little Superhero   2
1.2   A Big Estuary   3
1.3   A Frightening Character   4

Lesson 2   Synonyms, II **5**
2.1   A Great Tourist Attraction   6
2.2   An Aviation First   7
2.3   An Old Town   8

Lesson 3   Antonyms, I **9**
3.1   A Single President   10
3.2   Famous Rabbit's Line   11
3.3   An American First   12

Lesson 4   Antonyms, II **13**
4.1   Comic Strip Detective   14
4.2   Mark Twain   15
4.3   Great Words of a Great President   16

Lesson 5   Homographs, I **17**
5.1   An American Showman   18
5.2   A Many-Sided Figure   19
5.3   A Parliament   20

Lesson 6   Homographs, II **21**
6.1   Right to Left and Left to Right   22
6.2   Blood Pressure   23
6.3   A Computer Bug   24

Lesson 7 Homophones, I **25**

 7.1 A Man of Great Intellect and Talent 26

 7.2 A Surveyor's Tool 27

 7.3 Volcanic Rock with a Special Property 28

Lesson 8 Homophones, II **29**

 8.1 Paul Revere's Fellow Riders 30

 8.2 How Deep? 31

 8.3 The USS *Constitution* 32

Lesson 9 Easily Confused Words, I **33**

 9.1 A First for the Supreme Court 34

 9.2 Extinct Animals 35

 9.3 A Family Pet 36

Lesson 10 Easily Confused Words, II **37**

 10.1 Symbol of a Political Party 38

 10.2 A Somewhat Unpleasant Character 39

 10.3 An Uncommon Two-Term President 40

Lesson 11 Easily Confused Words, III **41**

 11.1 A Long Tail 42

 11.2 A Submarine First 43

 11.3 A First for a President 44

Lesson 12 Words with Latin Roots, I **45**

 12.1 Comets 46

 12.2 King Tut 47

 12.3 Uranus 48

Lesson 13 Words with Latin Roots, II **49**

 13.1 An Imitator 50

 13.2 A Barber's Son 51

 13.3 Internet Inventor 52

Lesson 14 Words with Greek Roots, I **53**

 14.1 Four Special Words 54

 14.2 A One-of-a-Kind State 55

 14.3 Volcano 56

Lesson 15 Words with Greek Roots, II **57**

 15.1 Canada 58

 15.2 A Story for All Ages 59

 15.3 Dolly the Sheep 60

Lesson 16   Prefixes, I..**61**
  16.1   First for a Postage Stamp 62
  16.2   Penguins 63
  16.3   Great Seal of the United States 64

Lesson 17   Prefixes, II...**65**
  17.1   Mercury 66
  17.2   Goldfish 67
  17.3   A Big Volcano 68

Lesson 18   Suffixes, I...**69**
  18.1   Colonial Newspaper Editor 70
  18.2   A Crayon Milestone 71
  18.3   A Forgotten Character 72

Lesson 19   Suffixes, II..**73**
  19.1   Play Ball! 74
  19.2   West of the Mississippi 75
  19.3   Milwaukee 76

Lesson 20   Words That Name, I...**77**
  20.1   An American Novelist 78
  20.2   Under the Sea 79
  20.3   An Unusual Snake 80

Lesson 21   Words That Name, II..**81**
  21.1   A Famous Rabbit 82
  21.2   Cracker Jack 83
  21.3   Breaking the Sound Barrier 84

Lesson 22   Words That Name, III...**85**
  22.1   Minnesota 86
  22.2   King Kong 87
  22.3   A Very Loud Animal 88

Lesson 23   Words That Name, IV...**89**
  23.1   An Archenemy 90
  23.2   Alabama 91
  23.3   A Chicago First 92

Lesson 24   Action Words, I..**93**
  24.1   A Candy Man 94
  24.2   A Different Method for Growing Plants 95
  24.3   The Three Musketeers 96

Lesson 25   Action Words, II..**97**
25.1   A Sneeze-Causing Plant   98
25.2   Candy Maker   99
25.3   Andromeda   100

Lesson 26   Action Words, III..**101**
26.1   The First Loser   102
26.2   An American Cookbook   103
26.3   Big News Via Telegraph   104

Lesson 27   Action Words, IV..**105**
27.1   Chimpanzees   106
27.2   Ohio   107
27.3   A First for the U.S. Congress   108

Lesson 28   Descriptive Words, I..**109**
28.1   In Pursuit of Atoms   110
28.2   Grenada   111
28.3   Cleaning the Coasts   112

Lesson 29   Descriptive Words, II...**113**
29.1   Your Lungs   114
29.2   A Cave Researcher   115
29.3   Teeth   116

Lesson 30   Descriptive Words, III..**117**
30.1   The Hairs on Your Head   118
30.2   A Book Collector   119
30.3   An Ancient City   120

Lesson 31   Descriptive Words, IV..**121**
31.1   Your Blood Vessels   122
31.2   A Secret   123
31.3   A Special Science   124

Lesson 32   Compound Words, I...**125**
32.1   Cartoon Sorcerer   126
32.2   First Televised Presidential Debate   127
32.3   The Stars in the Sky   128

Lesson 33   Compound Words, II..**129**
33.1   The Chipmunks   130
33.2   The First Moon Landing   131
33.3   The Wizard of Oz   132

Lesson 34   Words from Other Languages, I..................................**133**
   34.1   Electric Eels   134
   34.2   The Statue of Liberty   135
   34.3   Freshwater   136

Lesson 35   Words from Other Languages, II..................................**137**
   35.1   Foot Size   138
   35.2   A Fictional Detective   139
   35.3   Motion   140

Lesson 36   Words Based on Names..................................**141**
   36.1   The Top Three Elements   142
   36.2   Used the World Over   143
   36.3   The Tall and the Short   144

Lesson 37   Words for Readers and Writers..................................**145**
   37.1   Uncommon Presidents   146
   37.2   Driest and Lowest   147
   37.3   A Lot of Mackerel   148

Lesson 38   Math Words..................................**149**
   38.1   A Numbers Man   150
   38.2   Hamburger   151
   38.3   Roller Coaster   152

Lesson 39   Social Studies Words..................................**153**
   39.1   Your Muscles   154
   39.2   A Legendary Basketball Player   155
   39.3   A Presidential Resignation   156

Lesson 40   Science Words..................................**157**
   40.1   Moon Rocks   158
   40.2   Mount Rushmore   159
   40.3   Twinkies   160

Word List   161
Answer Key   165

About This Book

Words are the foundation of reading, speaking, and writing. It is through words that we share ideas and learn new things. Your understanding and use of words—your vocabulary—relate directly to learning. Students who have rich vocabularies usually do better in school than students whose vocabularies are poor.

The lessons in this book provide more than 450 words that are found in sixth, seventh, and eighth grade curriculums. The definitions of these words include more words that can expand your vocabulary even further. Many of the words throughout this book appear on standardized tests.

Practice Makes Perfect: Mastering Vocabulary can be a helpful resource for learning the meanings and uses of words. It can be used by both students and teachers. Students (working alone or with their parents) can complete the lessons, while teachers will find the materials of the book useful for classroom instruction.

Having a broad vocabulary is a key to being successful in school and beyond. It is my hope that this book will make your study of vocabulary an enjoyable experience.

How to Use This Book

*P*ractice Makes Perfect: Mastering Vocabulary contains forty lessons. Each lesson focuses on a particular type of word or word group and includes a list of words and three practice worksheets. An alphabetical list of the words in the lessons and an answer key for the worksheets conclude the book.

The first page of each lesson presents words you should know. Most lessons present ten words, but a few present more. For most lessons, words are shown with their part of speech, definition, and a sample sentence. A Vocabulary Tip is included at the bottom of the page. You should study the list of words and their definitions for each lesson before trying to do the worksheets. Use your dictionary to check the meanings of any words in the definitions that are new to you. Learning these words, along with the words presented in the lesson, will expand your vocabulary greatly.

The worksheets are designed to make learning vocabulary easy and fun. Each worksheet begins with a question that you can answer by completing the worksheet correctly. Try to complete the worksheets without looking back at the definitions of the list words. Look back only if you need help.

Completing the worksheets in this book will help you to expand your vocabulary. But there are many other ways you can learn new words and their meanings:

- Read. Reading builds vocabulary. Read different kinds of selections: novels, short stories, nonfiction books, and magazines. Make reading a habit.
- Use context clues to find the meanings of new words. You can often figure out the meaning of a word by the way it is used in a sentence. Look for clues in the following:
  ○ Examples that give the meaning of a new word
  ○ Familiar words and phrases that hint at the meaning of a new word
  ○ Phrases after new words that contain their definitions
  ○ Synonyms and antonyms that help you to understand the meanings of new words
- When necessary, use a dictionary to find the meanings of new words.
- When you learn a new word, note if it has multiple meanings. Many words do. Try to learn the different meanings of new words.

- Learn the meanings of prefixes and suffixes. Prefixes and suffixes alter the meanings of words. Use your understanding of prefixes and suffixes to help you understand the meanings of the words to which they are attached.
- When you learn a new word, repeat it and its meaning silently to yourself. Think of how the word is related to other words. This will help you to remember it.
- Think of a new word's synonyms and antonyms. This will broaden your understanding of the word.
- Write down new words and their meanings in a "New Words" notebook. Review your notebook from time to time to refresh your memory.
- Use a thesaurus to find the synonyms of words.
- Do word games such as crossword puzzles.
- Look for new words wherever you go, every day, and in every subject in school.

As soon as you learn new words, make them a part of your vocabulary. Use them in your speaking, reading, and writing.

MASTERING

Vocabulary

Synonyms, I

A synonym is a word that has the same, or nearly the same, meaning as another word.

1. adequate (adj): suitable; sufficient; satisfactory; enough; ample

   The replacement parts for the old lawn mower were <u>adequate</u>.

2. fickle (adj): changeable; capricious; erratic; whimsical

   Sara is <u>fickle</u> and constantly changes her mind.

3. humility (n): modesty; humbleness

   Peter's <u>humility</u> makes him one of the most respected students in school.

4. loathe (v): hate; detest; scorn; disdain

   I <u>loathe</u> snakes of any kind.

5. flamboyant (adj): showy; flashy; ostentatious

   Wearing a checkered shirt and striped pants, the comedian made a <u>flamboyant</u> entrance.

6. versatile (adj): resourceful; ingenious; talented

   Uncle Bob is <u>versatile</u> and can fix just about anything.

7. torrid (adj): hot; scorching; burning; broiling

   The <u>torrid</u> temperature of the desert was unbearable.

8. vicious (adj): cruel; ferocious; fierce; violent

   The <u>vicious</u> dog snarled and growled.

9. opponent (n): adversary; foe; antagonist; competitor

   My <u>opponent</u> for the tennis match was the former champion.

10. serene (adj): tranquil; pleasant; peaceful; composed

    We spent a <u>serene</u> afternoon in the park.

> **Vocabulary Tip**
>
> **L**earning the synonyms of words is an excellent way to build your vocabulary.

1.1 A Little Superhero

This superhero is associated with the words "Here I come to save the day." Who is he?

To answer the question, match each word on the left with its synonym on the right. Write the letter of each answer in the space above the word's number at the bottom of the page. You will need to divide the letters into words.

Words

1. vicious _Ferocious_
2. humility _modesty_
3. flamboyant _Showy_
4. adequate _Sufficient_
5. loathe _hate_
6. serene _tranquil_
7. torrid _Scorching_
8. versatile _ingenious_
9. opponent _adversary_
10. fickle _changeable_

Synonyms

U. tranquil

Y. scorching

E. sufficient

M. ingenious

O. showy

T. ferocious

I. changeable

H. hate

S. adversary

G. modesty

M	I	G	H	T	Y	M	O	U	S	E
8	10	2	5	1	7	8	3	6	9	4

1.2 A Big Estuary

This is the largest estuary in the United States. What is its name?

To answer the question, read each sentence below. Replace each underlined word with its synonym. Choose your answers from the words after each sentence. Write the letter of each answer in the space above its sentence number at the bottom of the page. You will need to divide the letters into words. Some letters are provided.

1. Roland came to the dance with a flamboyant red and purple coat.
   S. erratic   P. flashy   E. ample

2. We could not stop sweating in the torrid afternoon sun.
   A. scorching   I. ostentatious   U. capricious

3. The gladiator took his position in the arena and waited for his foe.
   N. scorn   T. versatile   S. opponent

4. The fickle woman could not decide which one of a dozen outfits to buy.
   O. serene   Y. talented   E. capricious

5. The barbarian leader was cruel in battle and offered no mercy.
   A. flamboyant   E. vicious   R. whimsical

6. I like to sleep late and loathe waking up early in the morning.
   E. hate   M. peaceful   O. satisfactory

7. The versatile tool contained a screwdriver, pliers, and scissors.
   A. ingenious   I. erratic   S. ample

8. Tom was confident he had packed sufficient food for the camping trip.
   S. pleasant   H. versatile   C. adequate

9. We had hoped to spend a serene day by the pool in our backyard, but it rained.
   H. tranquil   R. broiling   Q. changeable

10. Humility is a trait everyone should possess.
    E. Antagonist   Y. Modesty   T. Adequate

C	h	e	S	a	P	e	a	K	e	B	a Y
8	9	5	3	7	1	6	2		4		2 10

1.3 A Frightening Character

This character terrified Ichabod Crane in Washington Irving's story, "The Legend of Sleepy Hollow." Who was he?

To answer the question, complete each sentence with the correct word. Choose your answers from the words after the sentences. Write the letter of each answer in the space above its sentence number at the bottom of the page. You will need to divide the letters into words. One letter is provided.

1. The weather was ___fickle___ today with snow, rain, and sunshine.
2. The wizard transformed himself into a ___vicious___, fire-breathing dragon.
3. The ___torrid___ heat wave dried up rivers and destroyed crops.
4. Chad and his ___opponent___ in the wrestling tournament were well matched.
5. Roger is ___flamboyant___ and loves flashy clothes.
6. The two princes ___loathe___ each other because each wishes to be king.
7. Lauren is a ___versatile___ softball player who can play several positions.
8. We relaxed and enjoyed a ___serene___ day at the beach.
9. The ship brought ___adequate___ supplies for the colonists to survive the winter.
10. Kate accepted the award with grace and ___humility___.

Answers

O. vicious   S. versatile   L. fickle   H. serene   M. adequate

T. flamboyant   A. torrid   N. loathe   E. humility   D. opponent

T	h	e	H	e	a	d	l	e	s	s
5	8	10	8	10	3	4	1	10	7	7

h	a	R	s	e	m	a	n
8	2		7	10	9	3	6

4

Synonyms, II

A synonym is a word that has the same, or nearly the same, meaning as another word.

1. vigilant (adj): watchful; wary; alert

   Secret Service agents are <u>vigilant</u> in their duty to protect the president.

2. sensible (adj): astute; insightful; wise

   Anna is a <u>sensible</u> girl who always makes practical decisions.

3. absurd (adj): foolish; ridiculous; ludicrous; preposterous

   The story was so <u>absurd</u> that Shawn stopped reading after the first few pages.

4. cringe (v): flinch; shrink; cower; recoil

   I always <u>cringe</u> at the sight of needles.

5. inconspicuous (adj): unremarkable; unassuming; indistinct

   The undercover police officer was <u>inconspicuous</u> in his jeans and flannel shirt.

6. bountiful (adj): abundant; plentiful; generous; fruitful

   The settlers rejoiced in their <u>bountiful</u> harvest.

7. novice (n): beginner; trainee; apprentice; amateur

   Although Mandy was a <u>novice</u> at figure skating, she was learning quickly.

8. prior (adj): previous; earlier; preceding

   Having missed the <u>prior</u> math assignment, Jessica had trouble completing her homework.

9. invincible (adj): indomitable; unconquerable; invulnerable

   The king's knights were <u>invincible</u> in battle.

10. emphasize (v): stress; accentuate; feature

    My teachers always <u>emphasize</u> important ideas.

> **Vocabulary Tip**
>
> **A** thesaurus is a book that contains a list of words and their synonyms.

2.1 A Great Tourist Attraction

This place is considered to be a major tourist attraction. It is also considered to be the oldest tourist attraction in the United States. What is it?

To answer the question, find the synonym of each word below. Choose your answers from the choices that follow each word. Write the letter of each answer in the space above its line number at the bottom of the page. You will need to divide the letters into words. Some letters are provided.

1. bountiful: E. insightful   R. abundant   N. preceding

2. invincible: A. indomitable   I. flinch   S. cautious

3. absurd: I. indistinct   O. astute   A. ridiculous

4. emphasize: M. recoil   R. previous   L. stress

5. novice: G. beginner   A. wary   N. preposterous

6. cringe: I. flinch   E. stress   W. ludicrous

7. inconspicuous: T. invulnerable   S. unremarkable   H. foolish

8. prior: U. abundant   N. indistinct   L. previous

9. vigilant: L. foolish   R. unconquerable   N. watchful

10. sensible: N. unremarkable   F. astute   E. generous

N   i   a   g   A   r   A   f   a   k   l   S
9   6   2   5   1   10 3   8   4   7

Synonyms, II

6

© Gary Robert Muschla

2.2 An Aviation First

This woman became the United States Army's first female helicopter pilot. Who is she?

To answer the question, read each sentence below. Replace each underlined word with its synonym. Choose your answers from the words after each sentence. Write the letter of each answer in the space above its sentence number at the bottom of the page. You will need to divide the letters into words. One letter is provided.

1. Maria started taking dance lessons last year but still considers herself a novice.
   D. prior   L. beginner   R. vigilant

2. I cringe at the thought of telling Dad I broke a window in the garage.
   N. stress   R. cower   E. wary

3. Wearing a disguise, the prince was unassuming as he slipped out of the castle.
   Y. inconspicuous   S. invincible   N. sensible

4. Tim's explanation of why he had not finished his work was ridiculous.
   H. vigilant   Y. absurd   N. prior

5. At our family's Thanksgiving dinner, we enjoyed a bountiful feast.
   H. plentiful   M. preposterous   K. previous

6. The invincible castle guarded the countryside.
   S. alert   U. astute   A. unconquerable

7. During my presentation, I will emphasize the causes of the Civil War.
   R. insightful   P. stress   I. recoil

8. The sensible decision is to remain at home until the storm ends.
   E. wary   A. indistinct   S. wise

9. Sue Lin missed the earlier tryouts for the school play.
   L. prior   A. bountiful   R. astute

10. The palace's guards are watchful at their posts.
    E. sensible   U. vigilant   O. invincible

$\underline{S}$ $\underline{Q}$ $\underline{l}$ $\underline{l}$ $\underline{Y}$ $\underline{M}$ $\underline{U}$ $\underline{r}$ $\underline{P}$ $\underline{h}$ $\underline{Y}$
  8   6   1   9   4   10   2   7   5   3

Synonyms, II

2.3 An Old Town

1. Ty has been riding horses for only a few weeks and is still a ___novice___ at horseback riding.

2. Be sure to ___emphasize___ the major ideas in your report.

3. No one could stop the ___invincible___ invaders as they swept across the land.

4. A lot of students ___cringe___ when told they are getting homework during a holiday.

5. The ___inconspicuous___ envelope on the table contained a check for a million dollars.

6. The fertile land of the valley allowed farmers to grow ___bountiful___ crops.

7. The burglar's defense that he was a modern day Robin Hood was ___absurd___.

8. ___Sensible___ people think carefully before making important decisions.

9. When applying for a job, Jacob had to list his ___prior___ work experience.

10. The mother fox was ___vigilant___ as her cubs played outside the den.

Answers

S. absurd	A. vigilant	F. bountiful	U. novice	G. cringe
N. inconspicuous	O. invincible	I. emphasize	D. sensible	T. prior

S T   A u g u s t i n e   E,   f L o R i d a
7 9   10 1 4 1 7 9 2 5   6 3 2 8 10

Antonyms, I

An antonym is a word that has the opposite or about the opposite meaning of another word.

1. **facetious** (adj): playfully humorous; comical   Antonyms: serious; grave; solemn

   The audience laughed throughout the <u>facetious</u> play.

2. **notable** (adj): prominent or distinguished   Antonyms: unimportant; undistinguished; unknown

   Many <u>notable</u> authors attended the writers' conference.

3. **outlandish** (adj): very strange or unusual in manner or appearance; bizarre   Antonyms: ordinary; familiar; usual

   Reynaldo's rainbow won the prize for the most <u>outlandish</u> Halloween costume.

4. **apparent** (adj): easily seen or understood; obvious   Antonyms: doubtful; obscure; uncertain

   Becky's relief at the high grade on her test was <u>apparent</u>.

5. **gullible** (adj): easily deceived; unsuspecting   Antonyms: suspicious; wary; skeptical

   <u>Gullible</u> people often become the victims of fraud.

6. **formidable** (adj): arousing fear or alarm because of strength or power; intimidating   Antonyms: insignificant; powerless; weak

   The Spartans of ancient Greece were <u>formidable</u> warriors.

7. **casual** (adj): occurring by chance; not planned   Antonyms: intentional; planned; formal

   Our family enjoys <u>casual</u> activities on the weekends.

8. **efficient** (adj): acting or working with minimal waste; effective   Antonyms: inefficient; wasteful; unproductive

   Tom makes <u>efficient</u> use of his time and finishes his assignments quickly.

9. **logical** (adj): showing clear reason; rational   Antonyms: illogical; confused; irrational

   Elena developed her ideas for her report in a <u>logical</u> manner.

10. **extravagant** (adj): extremely lavish or abundant
    Antonyms: modest; restrained; thrifty

    Mia's parents gave her an <u>extravagant</u> sweet sixteen party.

Vocabulary Tip

When you learn the antonyms of words, you expand your vocabulary.

3.1 A Single President

This president was the only U.S. president never to marry. Who was he?

To answer the question, find the word for each definition below. Choose your answers from the words that follow each definition. Write the letter of each answer in the space above its definition number at the bottom of the page. You will need to divide the letters into words.

1. arousing fear or alarm because of strength or power
   E. apparent   U. formidable   S. extravagant

2. playfully humorous
   O. gullible   N. efficient   E. facetious

3. showing clear reason
   S. efficient   C. logical   I. formidable

4. extremely lavish or abundant
   S. extravagant   A. casual   R. apparent

5. acting or working with minimal waste
   H. efficient   J. formidable   W. facetious

6. easily deceived
   O. extravagant   S. outlandish   M. gullible

7. prominent or distinguished
   E. casual   N. notable   R. logical

8. very strange or unusual in manner or appearance
   N. gullible   B. outlandish   U. apparent

9. occurring by chance; not planned
   J. casual   E. logical   R. facetious

10. easily seen or understood
    L. outlandish   H. efficient   A. apparent

___ ___ ___ ___ ___ ___ ___ ___ ___ ___ ___ ___ ___
 9   10   6   2   4   8   1   3   5   10   7   10   7

Antonyms, I

10

3.2 Famous Rabbit's Line

Bugs Bunny is a cartoon favorite. What is his famous line?

To answer the question, match each word with its antonym. Write the letter of each answer in the space above the word's number at the bottom of the page. You will need to divide the letters into words.

Words

1. efficient _____

2. apparent _____

3. gullible _____

4. formidable _____

5. casual _____

6. facetious _____

7. extravagant _____

8. notable _____

9. logical _____

10. outlandish _____

Antonyms

T. obscure

H. intentional

P. unimportant

C. thrifty

U. wasteful

A. irrational

O. insignificant

S. serious

D. ordinary

W. suspicious

___ ___ ___ ___ ___ ___' ___ ___ ___ ___ ___ ___?
  9   5   3   5   9   2   6   1   8   10   4   7

Antonyms, I

© Gary Robert Muschla

3.3 An American First

Written by Harriet Beecher Stowe, this American novel was the first to sell over one million copies. What was its title?

To answer the question, correct the sentences below by replacing each underlined word with its antonym. Choose your answers from the words after the sentences. Write the letter of each answer in the space above its sentence number at the bottom of the page. You will need to divide the letters into words. Some letters are provided.

1. The use of robots has made the manufacturing process more <u>wasteful</u>.

2. A con artist can convince a <u>skeptical</u> person to buy just about anything.

3. The champions were a <u>weak</u> football team.

4. Being an experienced chess player, the next move was <u>uncertain</u> to James.

5. Lindsay was sure that the cost for the <u>modest</u> party was excessive.

6. The events of the enjoyable story built to a <u>confused</u> conclusion.

7. After wearing a suit to work all week, Sean likes to wear <u>formal</u> clothes during the weekend.

8. As an astronomer and scientist, Galileo made many <u>unimportant</u> discoveries.

9. Darren, who wants to be a comedy writer someday, is always telling <u>serious</u> stories.

10. Everyone was shocked at the <u>ordinary</u> sweater the usually shy Louis wore to school.

Answers

T. apparent	M. logical	N. facetious	U. outlandish	S. efficient
I. extravagant	A. gullible	L. formidable	C. casual	B. notable

__	__	__	__	E	__	O	__ '	__	__	__	__	__	__
10	9	7	3		4		6	1	7	2	8	5	9

Antonyms, II

An antonym is a word that has the opposite or about the opposite meaning of another word.

1. abolish (v): to do away with; end   Antonyms: establish; build; create

   The mayor plans to <u>abolish</u> fees in the downtown parking garage.

2. precise (adj): clearly expressed; definite   Antonyms: approximate; ambiguous; vague

   I took <u>precise</u> measurements before cutting the wood for the new shelves.

3. curtail (v): to cut short; reduce   Antonyms: expand; extend; lengthen

   Dad had to <u>curtail</u> his vacation because of an emergency at his office.

4. allegiance (n): loyalty to a nation, ruler, or cause; faithfulness   Antonyms: disloyalty; treachery; betrayal

   The knights swore <u>allegiance</u> to their new king.

5. sagacious (adj): possessing wisdom and sound judgment; intelligent   Antonyms: unwise; shortsighted; foolish

   The chief was a <u>sagacious</u> leader who was respected by his people.

6. reluctant (adj): unwilling; disinclined; unenthusiastic   Antonyms: willing; eager; enthusiastic

   Keisha is <u>reluctant</u> to join any more after-school clubs because of her busy schedule.

7. reputable (adj): having a good reputation; honorable   Antonyms: disreputable; unreliable; corrupt

   Tom is a <u>reputable</u> student and deserves to be class president.

8. substantial (adj): solid; strong; sizable   Antonyms: unsubstantial; fragile; weak; trifling

   The prosecutor presented <u>substantial</u> evidence during the trial.

9. customary (adj): commonly practiced; usual   Antonyms: unusual; irregular; uncommon

   In our town, it is <u>customary</u> to have a parade on the Fourth of July.

10. relevant (adj): relating to the matter at hand; pertinent   Antonyms: irrelevant; inappropriate; unrelated

    Jason made several <u>relevant</u> points during the debate.

> **Vocabulary Tip**
>
> **W**hen you learn a new word, think of some of its synonyms and antonyms.

13

4.1 Comic Strip Detective

Dick Tracy is a famous comic strip detective. What is the maiden name of Dick Tracy's wife?

To answer the question, find the word for each definition below. Choose your answers from the words after each definition. Write the letter of each answer in the space above its definition number at the bottom of the page. Some letters are provided.

1. commonly practiced
   S. customary   A. relevant   H. allegiance

2. possessing wisdom and sound judgment
   A. perceptive   I. substantial   E. sagacious

3. relating to the matter at hand
   T. relevant   N. precise   S. reputable

4. to cut short; reduce
   A. customary   E. curtail   Y. abolish

5. loyalty to a nation, ruler, or cause
   R. sagacious   S. allegiance   T. substantial

6. to do away with; end
   E. relevant   A. abolish   N. reluctant

7. having a good reputation
   R. reputable   H. allegiance   A. precise

8. solid; strong; sizable
   S. reluctant   B. sagacious   T. substantial

9. clearly expressed; definite
   C. customary   T. precise   M. abolish

10. unwilling; disinclined; unenthusiastic
    E. relevant   U. curtail   R. reluctant

__	E	__	__		__	__	U	__	H	__	__	__	__
8	5	1			9	7		4		2	6	10	3

4.2 Mark Twain

Mark Twain was the pseudonym of Samuel Clemens, a famous American author. The term *mark twain* is a Mississippi River phrase that refers to the depth of water. What does mark twain mean?

   To answer the question, match each word with its antonym. Write the letter of each answer in the space above the word's number at the bottom of the page. One letter is provided.

Words

1. customary _____
2. sagacious _____
3. relevant _____
4. reluctant _____
5. abolish _____
6. allegiance _____
7. reputable _____
8. substantial _____
9. curtail _____
10. precise _____

Antonyms

M. unrelated

W. disloyalty

A. shortsighted

E. fragile

H. unusual

O. corrupt

D. extend

F. ambiguous

P. establish

T. enthusiastic

$\frac{}{4}$ $\frac{}{6}$ $\frac{}{7}$ $\frac{}{10}$ $\frac{}{2}$ $\frac{}{4}$ $\frac{}{1}$ $\frac{}{7}$ $\frac{}{3}$ $\frac{S}{}$ $\frac{}{9}$ $\frac{}{8}$ $\frac{}{8}$ $\frac{}{5}$

4.3 Great Words of a Great President

In a famous speech after a great battle, this American president described democracy as ". . . government of the people, by the people, and for the people . . ." Who was he?

To answer the question, correct the sentences below by replacing each under-lined word with its antonym. Choose your answers from the words after the sentences. Write the letter of each answer in the space above its sentence number at the bottom of the page. You will need to divide the letters into words.

1. The town's <u>weak</u> flood walls easily held the rain-swollen river back.

2. Once it began snowing, the mayor decided to <u>extend</u> the meeting with the town council.

3. Rebecca is a shy person who is <u>willing</u> to speak in front of large groups.

4. My grandfather was a <u>foolish</u> man who I could always go to for sound advice.

5. The citizens pledged <u>disloyalty</u> to their country.

6. We always buy products from <u>unreliable</u> companies.

7. When dining out, it is <u>uncommon</u> to "tip" a waiter or waitress for good service.

8. The teacher cautioned her students to only include <u>unrelated</u> facts in their reports.

9. Congress should act to <u>create</u> old, outdated laws.

10. You must make <u>approximate</u> calculations to find the exact answer to a math problem.

Answers

M. reluctant	B. customary	C. allegiance	N. relevant	O. substantial
H. reputable	I. curtail	A. abolish	L. precise	R. sagacious

___ ___ ___ ___ ___ ___ ___ ___ ___ ___ ___ ___ ___ ___
 9   7   4   9   6   9   3 10   2   8   5   1 10   8

Homographs, I

Homographs are words that have the same spelling but different meanings and origins. Although most homographs sound alike, some have different pronunciations.

1. bluff (n): a steep bank, cliff, or headland

   bluff (v): to mislead, deceive, or fool

2. incense (in´sĕns´) (n): a substance that burns with a pleasant odor

   incense (in sĕns´) (v): to make angry; to infuriate

3. poach (v): to cook in a hot or boiling liquid

   poach (v): to trespass in order to take fish or game

4. flounder (n): a kind of fish

   flounder (v): to move in a struggling, clumsy manner

5. object (ŏb´ jĭkt, -jĕkt´) (n): a thing

   object (əb jĕkt´) (v): to protest

6. stoop (n): a small porch, staircase, or platform leading to the entrance of a building

   stoop (v): to bend forward from the waist

7. shingles (n): roofing materials

   shingles (n): a viral disease

8. refrain (n): a repeated part of a song or poem

   refrain (v): to hold back

9. staple (n): a principal item or material

   staple (n): a u-shaped metal fastener

   staple (v): to fasten by means of a staple

10. rifle (n): a long-barreled gun designed to be fired from the shoulder

    rifle (v): to ransack or search with the purpose of stealing

---

Vocabulary Tip

Many words in English have multiple meanings. These words should not be confused with homographs.

5.1 An American Showman

P. T. Barnum was an American showman best known for establishing a circus. What was Barnum's circus called?

To answer the question, match each definition on the left with the correct homograph on the right. Write the letter of each answer in the space above its definition number at the bottom of the page. You will need to divide the letters into words.

Definitions

1. to trespass in order to take fish or game _____

2. a viral disease _____

3. a principal item or material _____

4. a steep bank, cliff, or headland _____

5. to bend forward from the waist _____

6. a substance that burns with a pleasant odor _____

7. to hold back _____

8. to move in a struggling, clumsy manner _____

9. to ransack or search with the purpose of stealing _____

10. to protest _____

Homographs

W. bluff

G. refrain

T. rifle

O. shingles

E. flounder

A. staple

S. poach

N. incense

H. object

R. stoop

| — | — | — | — | — | — | — | — | — | — | — | — | — | — |
| 9 | 10 | 8 | 7 | 5 | 8 | 3 | 9 | 8 | 1 | 9 | 1 | 10 | 2 | 4 |

| — | — | — | — | — | — | — |
| 2 | 6 | 8 | 3 | 5 | 9 | 10 |

5.2 A Many-Sided Figure

This geometric figure has twenty faces. What is it called?

To answer the question, complete each sentence with the correct word. Choose your answers from the words after the sentences. Write the letter of each answer in the space above its sentence number at the bottom of the page.

1. My father and I plan to _____ the fish we catch in melted butter.

2. The fortune teller's room had a rich smell of _____.

3. The puppy was so small that I had to _____ way down to pick it up.

4. My grandfather recently was ill with _____.

5. I went fishing yesterday and caught a _____.

6. After climbing to the top of the _____, we had a fine view of the valley.

7. Even though my little brother may hit me when he is mad, I _____ from hitting him.

8. The thief had just begun to _____ through the jewelry box when the police arrived.

9. Grain is a _____ for people around the world.

10. Thomas believes it is the duty of good citizens to _____ to unfair laws.

Answers

D. rifle   N. stoop   R. bluff   S. object   I. shingles
E. poach   H. flounder   C. refrain   A. incense   O. staple

— — — — — — — — — — —
4   7   9   10   2   5   1   8   6   9   3

5.3 A Parliament

The word *parliament* is most commonly used to name a legislative body within a country. The word also refers to this animal. What animal is this?

To answer the question, read each sentence below. Match the underlined word with its definition. Choose your answers from the definitions after the sentences. Not all of the definitions will be used. Write the letter of each answer in the space above its sentence number at the bottom of the page. You will need to divide the letters into words.

1. Sammi used a broom to sweep the snow off the stoop.

2. I like to sing along with this refrain.

3. Will tried to bluff the other card players into thinking he had a winning hand.

4. We replaced the shingles on our house.

5. I decided to poach an egg for breakfast.

6. Sara could not determine what the strange object in the sky was.

7. Mom cooked flounder for dinner.

8. The rebels' victories incense the evil prince.

9. I was careless and almost put a staple in my finger.

10. My father added a new rifle to his collection.

Answers

H. to bend forward
L. to make angry
U. a kind of fish
F. roofing materials
E. to hold back
P. a small porch
A. a thing
G. to mislead
M. a viral disease
T. to protest
J. a steep bank

V. to ransack
B. a principal item or material
I. a steep bank, cliff, or headland
N. a substance that burns with a pleasant odor
S. a repeated part of a song or poem
C. to move in a struggling or clumsy manner
W. to cook in a hot or boiling liquid
O. a u-shaped metal fastener
R. a long-barreled gun designed to be fired from the shoulder

___ ___ ___ ___ ___ ___ ___ ___ ___ ___ ___ ___
6   3   10   9   7   1   9   4   9   5   8   2

Homographs, I

Homographs, II

Homographs are words that have the same spelling but different meanings and origins. Although most homographs sound alike, some have different pronunciations.

1. console (kŏn´ sōl´) (n): a type of cabinet or table

   console (kən sōl´) (v): to provide comfort to ease grief

2. racket (n): a paddle used in sports such as tennis

   racket (n): an uproar; noise

3. launch (n): an open boat

   launch (n): the act of sending off; (v): to start or send off

4. husky (n): a sled dog

   husky (adj): rugged and strong

5. lumber (n): wood sawed into boards; timber

   lumber (v): to walk or move heavily or clumsily

6. hamper (n): a basket or container used to store dirty laundry

   hamper (v): to slow the movement of

7. maroon (n): a dark reddish brown color

   maroon (v): to leave a person on a deserted island or coast

8. invalid (īn´ və lĭd) (n): a chronically ill or disabled person

   invalid (ĭn văl´ ĭd) (adj): not valid; null

9. reel (n): a spool or device for winding

   reel (v): to be thrown back or off balance

10. stern (n): rear part of a ship

    stern (adj): strict, harsh, or unyielding; inflexible

Vocabulary Tip

Heteronyms are homographs that have different pronunciations.

6.1 Right to Left and Left to Right

Words, phrases, and numbers that are read the same from left to right as they are from right to left have a special name. What is this name?

To answer the question, match each definition on the left with the correct homograph on the right. Write the letter of each answer in the space above its definition number at the bottom of the page.

Definitions   **Homographs**

1. a basket or container for storing dirty laundry _____   N. invalid

2. not valid; null _____   E. console

3. an uproar; noise _____   M. maroon

4. to provide comfort to ease grief _____   L. launch

5. a spool or device for winding _____   I. stern

6. a dark reddish brown color _____   O. hamper

7. an open boat _____   D. husky

8. a sled dog _____   R. racket

9. to walk or move heavily or clumsily _____   A. reel

10. strict, harsh, or unyielding; inflexible _____   P. lumber

___   ___   ___   ___   ___   ___   ___   ___   ___   ___
 9   5   7   10   2   8   3   1   6   4

6.2 Blood Pressure

A doctor or nurse uses this instrument to measure your blood pressure. What is it called?

To answer the question, complete each sentence with the correct word. Choose your answers from the words after the sentences. Write the letter of each answer in the space above its sentence number at the bottom of the page. Some letters are provided.

1. The explorer was a big, _____ man who had traveled throughout the frontier.

2. Erica stores her DVDs on the top shelf in the _____.

3. Chris bought a new _____ for the tennis tournament.

4. My neighbor never fully recovered from an accident and is an _____.

5. Walking into the closed glass door caused Martin to _____.

6. From the _____ of the ship we watched the dock fade into the distance.

7. The coming snowstorm is likely to _____ travel throughout the state.

8. Alberto loaded the _____ for the new deck onto his truck.

9. The pirate captain ordered the crew to _____ the prisoner on the deserted island.

10. The _____ of the rocket was a breathtaking sight.

Answers

P. racket	S. maroon	N. husky	T. stern	H. invalid
O. hamper	R. reel	M. launch	E. lumber	Y. console

__ __ __ __ G__ __ __ __ A__ __ __ __ __ __ __ __
9 3 4 2   10 7 10   1 7 10 8 6 8 5

Homographs, II

6.3 A Computer Bug

In 1947, after a moth was found in a computer circuit, this woman is believed to have coined the term "bug" for a computer glitch. Who was she?

To answer the question, read each sentence below. Match the underlined word with its definition. Choose your answers from the definitions after the sentences. Not all of the definitions will be used. Write the letter of each answer in the space above its sentence number at the bottom of the page. One letter is provided.

1. After their old cat died, Sheryl tried to <u>console</u> her little sister.

2. Mom always reminds me to put my dirty clothes in the <u>hamper</u>.

3. Jonathan received a new fishing pole and <u>reel</u> for his birthday.

4. My mother got annoyed with us because we were making a <u>racket</u>.

5. Mr. Wallace is a <u>stern</u> teacher.

6. Kelly's new sweater is <u>maroon</u> and gray.

7. Our school plans to <u>launch</u> a new reading program.

8. The mountain guide was a <u>husky</u> man.

9. The free ticket was <u>invalid</u> because its time limit had expired.

10. The bear stood up on its hind feet and started to <u>lumber</u> toward us.

Answers

C. an uproar; noise
Q. wood sawed into boards
F. an open boat
S. a sled dog
A. to start or send off
O. rugged and strong
E. not valid; null
W. a type of cabinet
N. to slow the movement of
R. to walk or move heavily or clumsily

M. a spool or device for winding
L. rear part of a ship
V. a chronically ill or disabled person
T. to be thrown back or off balance
Y. to provide comfort to ease grief
G. strict, harsh, or unyielding
H. a dark reddish brown color
I. to leave a person on a deserted island
P. a basket or container for dirty laundry
J. a paddle used in sports such as tennis

<u>__</u> <u>__</u> <u>__</u> <u>__</u> <u>__</u>   <u>U</u>   <u>__</u> <u>__</u> <u>__</u> <u>__</u>   <u>__</u> <u>__</u> <u>__</u> <u>__</u> <u>__</u> <u>__</u>
5 10 7 4 9   3   10 10 7 1   6 8 2 2 9 10

Homophones, I

Homophones are words that sound alike but have different meanings and spellings.

1. leased (v): rented

   least (adj): lowest in importance; smallest

2. borough (n): a town

   burro (n): a donkey

   burrow (n): a hole or tunnel dug by an animal; (v): to dig

3. council (n): an administrative or legislative body

   counsel (n): advice or guidance; (v): to advise

4. foreword (n): a preface or introduction to a book

   forward (adv): toward the front; (adj): at, near, or part of the front

5. bazaar (n): a market or fair

   bizarre (adj): outlandish; unconventional; eccentric; odd

6. straight (adj): extending in the same direction without curves

   strait (n): a narrow channel of water joining two larger bodies of water

7. incite (v): to stir up or provoke

   insight (n): the ability to understand the nature of things; understanding

8. stationary (adj): not moving

   stationery (n): writing paper and envelopes

9. plait (n): a braid, especially of hair; (v): to braid

   plate (n): a dish

10. profit (n): a gain or benefit; (v): to make a gain

    prophet (n): a person who speaks by divine inspiration; a seer

Vocabulary Tip

Proofread writing closely to avoid misusing homophones.

7.1 A Man of Great Intellect and Talent

Because of his accomplishments as an artist, sculptor, architect, engineer, and scientist, this man is considered to be one of history's towering figures. One of his greatest paintings was the *Mona Lisa*. Who was he?

To answer the question, match each definition on the left with the correct homophone on the right. Write the letter of each answer in the space above its definition number at the bottom of the page. Not all answers will be used.

Definitions

1. the ability to understand the nature of things _____

2. a town _____

3. an introduction to a book _____

4. lowest in importance _____

5. a gain or benefit _____

6. to advise _____

7. a narrow channel of water _____

8. not moving _____

9. a braid (of hair) _____

10. a market or fair _____

Homophones

Y. leased	N. least
H. prophet	O. profit
V. counsel	J. council
K. bizarre	D. bazaar
M. stationery	L. stationary
U. incite	R. insight
C. foreword	S. forward
A. strait	G. straight
E. borough	T. burrow
I. plait	W. plate

__ __ __ __ __ __ __ __   __ __   __ __ __ __ __
8 2 5 4 7 1 10 5   10 7   6 9 4 3 9

7.2 A Surveyor's Tool

This instrument contains a small mounted telescope. Surveyors use it to take precise measurements of angles. What is it called?

To find the answer, read each sentence below. Find the word that has a similar meaning to each underlined word or phrase. Choose your answers from the words after each sentence. Write the letter of each answer in the space above its sentence number at the bottom of the page.

1. The town's administrative body discussed the Memorial Day Parade.
   O. council   E. counsel

2. As the use of e-mail increases, the use of writing paper for letters decreases.
   A. stationary   O. stationery

3. I accidently broke a dish when setting the table.
   U. plait   I. plate

4. The inventor was a pleasant but eccentric man.
   M. bazaar   D. bizarre

5. Our family rented a house at the Jersey shore for the summer.
   E. leased   N. least

6. Danny's lawn mowing service made a significant gain this year.
   E. profit   A. prophet

7. The captain steered the boat into the narrow channel.
   R. straight   H. strait

8. The rabbit hid in his hole until the fox left.
   E. burro   T. burrow

9. Poking a beehive with a stick will stir up the bees.
   T. incite   C. insight

10. Stacy stepped toward the front of the room to receive her award.
    L. forward   S. foreword

___ ___ ___ ___ ___ ___ ___ ___ ___ ___
 9   7   6   2   4   1   10   3   8   5

7.3 Volcanic Rock with a Special Property

Pumice is a volcanic rock. It is the only rock that has this property. What can pumice do that no other rock can?

To answer the question, read each sentence below. If the underlined word is used correctly, write the letter for correct in the space above its sentence number at the bottom of the page. If the underlined word is not used correctly, write the letter for incorrect. You will need to divide the letters into words.

1. For math, we had to write decimals in order from <u>leased</u> to greatest.
   U. correct   I. incorrect

2. When we were on vacation, we went to a <u>bizarre</u> and bought souvenirs.
   D. correct   R. incorrect

3. When I have a problem, I can count on my older sister to give me good <u>council</u>.
   I. correct   O. incorrect

4. The sign said "Entering the <u>Borough</u> of Jefferson."
   A. correct   O. incorrect

5. The evil duke hoped to <u>incite</u> the people to rebellion against the king.
   E. correct   U. incorrect

6. The princess wore her hair in a long <u>plate</u>.
   R. correct   N. incorrect

7. The <u>profit</u> spoke of his visions for the coming new age.
   L. correct   W. incorrect

8. The <u>stationary</u> storm brought rain to the area for days.
   T. correct   I. incorrect

9. The <u>straight</u> road stretched across the prairie for miles.
   F. correct   T. incorrect

10. The <u>foreword</u> of a book serves as an introduction.
    L. correct   H. incorrect

___ ___ ___ ___ ___ ___ ___ ___ ___ ___ ___ ___
9   10   3   4   8   1   6   7   4   8   5   2

Homophones, II

Homophones are words that sound alike but have different meanings and spellings.

1. gorilla (n): a large ape

   guerrilla (n): a member of an irregular army

2. discreet (adj): tactful or prudent, especially when dealing with others

   discrete (adj): distinct or separate

3. patience (n): having the capacity for calm endurance; composure

   patients (n): people undergoing medical treatment

4. cymbal (n): a musical instrument (one of a pair of brass plates)

   symbol (n): something that represents another thing

5. attendance (n): the act of being present; presence

   attendants (n): persons who wait on or escort others; servants

6. lichen (n): a fungus

   liken (v): to show as being similar; compare

7. capital (n): a town or city that is the seat of a government; (n): wealth in the form of money or property

   capitol (n): a building in which a state legislature meets

   Capitol (n): the building of the United States Congress

8. cite (v): to quote an authority or example

   sight (n): the ability to see; (v): to see

   site (n): location

9. ascent (n): the act or process of moving upward; rise; climb

   assent (v): to agree

10. instance (n): an example

    instants (n): brief moments of time

Vocabulary Tip

Always pay close attention to the meanings of homophones and commit their meanings to memory.

8.1 Paul Revere's Fellow Riders

Two men accompanied Paul Revere on the night he rode to warn the colonists that the British were coming. One of these men was William Dawes. Who was the other?

To answer the question, match each definition on the left with the correct homophone on the right. Write the letter of each answer in the space above its definition number at the bottom of the page. Not all answers will be used. One letter is provided.

Definitions

1. the act of being present; presence _____

2. the ability to see _____

3. the act or process of moving upward _____

4. tactful or prudent _____

5. to show as similar; compare _____

6. a musical instrument _____

7. a large ape _____

8. an example _____

9. wealth in the form of money or property _____

10. people undergoing medical treatment _____

Homophones

U. ascent   Y. assent

B. symbol   P. cymbal

W. lichen   L. liken

O. sight   K. site

I. instants   M. instance

T. patients   G. patience

A. attendance   C. attendants

N. capitol   E. capital

V. guerrilla   S. gorilla

R. discreet   H. discrete

___ ___ ___ ___ ___ ___   ___ ___ ___ ___ _C_ ___ ___ ___
 7   1   8   3   9   5   6   4   9   7   2 10 10

8.2 How Deep?

This instrument is used to measure the depth of water. What is it called?
   To answer the question, complete each sentence with the correct word. Choose your answers from the words after each sentence. Write the letter of each answer in the space above its sentence number at the bottom of the page.

1. The painting was composed of numerous _____ geometric figures.
   O. discrete   E. discreet

2. The American flag is a _____ of the United States.
   T. symbol   R. cymbal

3. The five senses are _____ , hearing, touch, taste, and smell.
   U. site   E. sight

4. The city of Trenton is the _____ of New Jersey.
   H. capital   R. capitol

5. Only a few _____ passed between the flash of lightning and blast of thunder.
   S. instance   R. instants

6. Watching the long _____ of the roller coaster, I decided not to ride it.
   A. ascent   I. assent

7. It is easy to _____ wolves to dogs because of their similarities.
   E. liken   U. lichen

8. _____ at the championship game broke the previous record.
   S. Attendants   B. Attendance

9. _____ is a trait everyone should have.
   T. Patience   D. Patients

10. The man became a _____ in order to fight for the freedom of his country.
   C. gorilla   M. guerrilla

___ ___ ___ ___ ___ ___ ___ ___ ___ ___
 8   6   2   4   1   10   3   9   7   5

Homophones, II

8.3 The USS *Constitution*

The USS *Constitution* was commissioned in 1798. The ship won many battles and is one of the most famous ships in the history of the United States Navy. What is its nickname?

To answer the question, read each sentence below. If the underlined word is used correctly, write the letter for correct in the space above its sentence number at the bottom of the page. If the underlined word is not used correctly, write the letter for incorrect. You will need to divide the letters into words. Some letters are provided.

1. The parking <u>attendants</u> directed visitors where to park their cars.
   I. correct   E. incorrect

2. A flag with a skull and crossbones is a <u>cymbal</u> of pirates.
   U. correct   E. incorrect

3. Jaywalking is an <u>instance</u> of ignoring rules of safety.
   O. correct   R. incorrect

4. Tim has the <u>capitol</u> to expand his business.
   D. correct   S. incorrect

5. The <u>site</u> of the ancient temple was high in the mountains.
   N. correct   T. incorrect

6. Melissa is an energetic child who lacks <u>patients</u>.
   R. correct   D. incorrect

7. The <u>assent</u> of the elevator abruptly stopped.
   I. correct   D. incorrect

8. The natural habitat of the <u>gorilla</u> is slowly being destroyed.
   R. correct   M. incorrect

9. Mrs. Carter is a <u>discrete</u> person, who is always tactful with others.
   U. correct   L. incorrect

10. A <u>lichen</u> is a fungus that often grows in harsh environments.
    S. correct   M. incorrect

<u> </u> <u> </u> <u> </u> <u> </u> <u> </u> <u>O</u> <u> </u> <u> </u> <u>I</u> <u> </u> <u> </u> <u> </u>
3   9   7   1   8   5   10   6   2   4

Homophones, II

Easily Confused Words, I

Because they have similar sounds or spellings—but different meanings—some words are easily confused.

1. conscience (n): having a sense of right and wrong
   conscious (adj): being aware

2. personal (adj): private
   personnel (n): a group of people employed by a business or organization

3. allusion (n): an indirect reference
   illusion (n): a false vision of reality

4. precede (v): to go before
   proceed (v): to go forward; to move in an orderly manner

5. perpetrate (v): to be guilty of; to commit
   perpetuate (v): to prolong the existence of; to cause to be remembered

6. veracious (adj): truthful; honest
   voracious (adj): having a great appetite for food or pursuit of an activity; ravenous

7. contagious (adj): spread by contact; catchy
   contiguous (adj): sharing an edge or border; nearby

8. continual (adj): repeated regularly
   continuous (adj): uninterrupted; ceaseless

9. expand (v): to increase in size
   expend (v): to spend; to consume or use up

10. ingenious (adj): clever; skillful; resourceful
    ingenuous (adj): unsophisticated; straightforward; artless

> **Vocabulary Tip**
>
> **U**nderstanding the meanings of easily confused words can help you to avoid making mistakes with them.

9.1 A First for the Supreme Court

This person was the first woman to serve as a justice on the Supreme Court of the United States. Who was she?

To answer the question, match each definition with its word. Choose your answers from the words that follow each definition. Write the letter of each answer in the space above its definition number at the bottom of the page. Some letters are provided.

1. to be guilty of; to commit
   R. perpetrate   S. perpetuate

2. to spend; to consume or use up
   E. expand   O. expend

3. truthful; honest
   C. veracious   M. voracious

4. uninterrupted; ceaseless
   L. continual   D. continuous

5. being aware
   R. conscience   N. conscious

6. clever; skillful; resourceful
   A. ingenuous   O. ingenious

7. sharing an edge or border; nearby
   D. contiguous   S. contagious

8. an indirect reference
   N. allusion   L. illusion

9. to go before
   S. precede   T. proceed

10. a group of people employed by a business or organization
   E. personal   Y. personnel

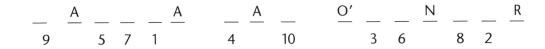

_	A	_	_	_	A	_	A	_	O'	_	_	N	_	_	R
9		5	7	1		4		10		3	6		8	2	

9.2 Extinct Animals

By far, most of the animal species that have lived on Earth are extinct. About what percent of all the animals that have ever lived on our planet are extinct?

To answer the question, complete each sentence with the correct word. Choose your answers from the words after each sentence. Write the letter of each answer in the space above its sentence number at the bottom of the page.

1. During fire drills, students are to _____ quickly to the nearest exit.
   O. precede   I. proceed

2. Having not eaten all day, I was _____ by dinnertime.
   Y. veracious   T. voracious

3. Influenza is a very _____ illness.
   Y. contagious   E. contiguous

4. Heat causes matter to _____ and take up more space.
   R. expend   E. expand

5. Uncle James is an _____ man who will tell you exactly what he thinks.
   I. ingenuous   O. ingenious

6. The _____ updates kept people informed of the hurricane's position.
   E. continual   R. continuous

7. Most people consider a diary to be a _____ possession.
   U. personnel   N. personal

8. The magician used an _____ to trick his audience.
   N. illusion   F. allusion

9. Listening to your _____ can help you to do the right thing.
   N. conscience   T. conscious

10. The memorial will _____ the heroic acts of firefighters.
    U. perpetrate   N. perpetuate

___   ___   ___   ___   ___   ___   -   ___   ___   ___   ___
 9   5   10   6   2   3   8   1   7   4

9.3 A Family Pet

In this cartoon TV show, the family's pet was named Dino. What was the name of the show?

To answer the question, read each sentence below. If the underlined word is used correctly, write the letter for correct in the space above its sentence number at the bottom of the page. If the underlined word is not used correctly, write the letter for incorrect. You will need to divide the letters into words. Some letters are provided.

1. The <u>continuous</u> rain resulted in severe flooding.
   N. correct   O. incorrect

2. The <u>ingenious</u> child put the complex puzzle together easily.
   E. correct   N. incorrect

3. Despite the seriousness of the accident, the driver of the car remained <u>conscience</u>.
   U. correct   E. incorrect

4. During a marathon, runners <u>expend</u> a tremendous amount of energy.
   H. correct   O. incorrect

5. Toni is a <u>veracious</u> reader who finishes at least two books every week.
   P. correct   I. incorrect

6. The directions said to turn right at the corner and <u>precede</u> west for three miles.
   R. correct   T. incorrect

7. Every employee at the company had a <u>personnel</u> parking space.
   I. correct   T. incorrect

8. The doctor told Sharyn that the rash on her arm was not <u>contagious</u>.
   F. correct   N. incorrect

9. The monster of the lake was an <u>allusion</u> caused by the mist.
   S. correct   T. incorrect

10. The new observatory will <u>perpetuate</u> its founder's love of astronomy.
    O. correct   A. incorrect

___ ___ ___ ___ __L__ __N__ __S__ ___ ___ ___ __S__
 9   4   3   8   5   7   6   10   1   2

Easily Confused Words. I

© Gary Robert Muschla

36

Easily Confused Words, II

Because they have similar sounds or spellings—but different meanings—some words are easily confused.

1. incredible (adj): too improbable to be believed; unbelievable
   incredulous (adj): unbelieving; skeptical

2. erasable (adj): removable by rubbing or scraping
   irascible (adj): easily angered

3. disinterested (adj): free of bias; impartial
   uninterested (adj): not paying attention; indifferent; not interested

4. confidant (n): a friend or advisor
   confident (adj): certain; sure; assured

5. adverse (adj): contrary to one's interests; opposing
   averse (adj): having an unfavorable feeling toward; disinclined

6. click (n): a short, sharp sound
   clique (n): a small, exclusive group

7. eminent (adj): well known; prominent
   imminent (adj): about to happen; impending

8. deference (n): courteous yielding to another; respect
   difference (n): dissimilarity; unlikeness

9. appraise (v): to evaluate; to set a value on
   apprise (v): to inform

10. emerge (v): to rise out of
    immerge (v): to submerge or disappear in liquid

> **Vocabulary Tip**
>
> **L**earning the pronunciations and spellings of easily confused words will help you to recognize and use them correctly.

10.1 Symbol of a Political Party

The elephant is often considered to be an animal of great size, intelligence, strength, and dignity. Starting in the 1870s, this man popularized the elephant as a symbol of the Republican Party. Who was he?

To answer the question, match each definition with its word. Choose your answers from the words that follow each definition. Write the letter of each answer in the space above its definition number at the bottom of the page.

1. courteous yielding to another; respect
   E. difference   A. deference

2. to submerge or disappear in a liquid
   O. immerge   A. emerge

3. free of bias; impartial
   S. disinterested   R. uninterested

4. contrary to one's interests; opposing
   D. averse   T. adverse

5. to inform
   W. appraise   T. apprise

6. a friend or advisor
   S. confidant   R. confident

7. unbelieving; skeptical
   A. incredulous   E. incredible

8. a short, sharp sound
   B. clique   N. click

9. about to happen; impending
   H. imminent   A. eminent

10. removable by rubbing or scraping
    L. irascible   M. erasable

___ ___ ___ ___ ___ ___   ___ ___ ___ ___
 5   9   2   10 7   3   8   1   6   4

10.2 A Somewhat Unpleasant Character

This Muppet lives in a garbage can. Who is he?

To answer the question, complete each sentence with the correct word. Choose your answers from the words after each sentence. Write the letter of each answer in the space above its sentence number at the bottom of the page. You will need to divide the letters into words.

1. After studying for the test, Jasmine was _____ she would do well.
   T. confident   M. confidant

2. The _____ doctor was honored for his long service to the town.
   I. imminent   A. eminent

3. We watched the whale _____ from the water, leap, and then dive back in.
   O. immerge   E. emerge

4. The toddler was _____ in his new toy and played with his old ones.
   U. uninterested   T. disinterested

5. Jack's story of how the wind blew his homework away was _____.
   O. incredible   K. incredulous

6. Mr. Bartley is a cranky, _____ fellow.
   N. erasable   R. irascible

7. Whenever he speaks on his phone, Nathan hears an annoying _____.
   G. click   M. clique

8. The only _____ between the twins is the color of their glasses.
   E. deference   C. difference

9. Leah was _____ to running for student council because of her heavy schedule.
   E. adverse   S. averse

10. Teachers met with parents to _____ them of the new math program.
    H. apprise   T. appraise

| __ | __ | __ | __ | __ | __ | __ | __ | __ | __ | __ | __ | __ | __ |
| 5 | 9 | 8 | 2 | 6 | 1 | 10 | 3 | 7 | 6 | 5 | 4 | 8 | 10 |

10.3 An Uncommon Two-Term President

This president is the only U.S. president to have served two nonconsecutive terms in office. Who was he?

To answer the question, read each sentence below. Replace each underlined word or phrase with the word or phrase that has a similar meaning. Choose your answers from the words after each sentence. Write the letter of each answer in the space above its sentence number at the bottom of the page. You will need to divide the letters into words.

1. After the accident an insurance agent came to <u>evaluate</u> the damage to our car.
   A. appraise   T. apprise

2. I had seen the movie and knew that a creature would <u>rise out of</u> the swamp.
   O. emerge from   S. immerge from

3. Darcie has many friends and refuses to be a part of any <u>small, exclusive group</u>.
   O. click   N. clique

4. The wizard was also the king's <u>friend and advisor</u>.
   W. confident   C. confidant

5. The best judge of any contest is <u>an impartial</u> judge.
   V. a disinterested   R. an uninterested

6. Some animals, such as wild boars, are <u>easily angered</u>.
   N. erasable   D. irascible

7. The weather bulletin reported that a severe thunderstorm was <u>impending</u>.
   E. eminent   R. imminent

8. In our family the children treat their elders with <u>respect</u>.
   L. deference   A. difference

9. When my brother told me he had found a treasure map, I was <u>skeptical</u>.
   G. incredulous   T. incredible

10. Brittany is <u>disinclined</u> to eating foods with hot sauces.
    I. adverse   E. averse

___ ___ ___ ___ ___ ___ ___ ___ ___ ___ ___ ___ ___ ___ ___
9   7   2   5   10   7   4   8   10   5   10   8   1   3   6

Easily Confused Words, III

Because they have similar sounds or spellings—but different meanings—some words are easily confused.

1. respectably (adv): in a manner meriting respect

   respectively (adv): singly in the designated order

   respectfully (adv): in a proper, courteous, or respectful manner

2. elicit (v): to draw out; to evoke

   illicit (adj): unlawful

3. infer (v): to conclude from evidence; to deduce

   imply (v): to suggest or express indirectly; to hint

4. disburse (v): to pay out

   disperse (v): to scatter

5. indigent (adj): lacking the means for subsistence; poor; impoverished

   indignant (adj): very angry; incensed

6. anecdote (n): a short, amusing story

   antidote (n): a substance to counteract the effects of poison

7. eligible (adj): qualified; suitable

   illegible (adj): not able to be read; not decipherable

8. access (n): a means of approaching; passage

   excess (n): an amount beyond sufficient; surplus; (adj): being more than is usual

9. discomfit (v): to frustrate; to disconcert

   discomfort (n): distress; uneasiness; annoyance

10. elusive (adj): difficult to catch; hard to describe

    illusive (adj): having the nature of an illusion; misleading; illusory

---

Vocabulary Tip

Be sure to use easily confused words correctly when speaking and writing.

11.1 A Long Tail

1. a means of approaching; passage
   E. access   H. excess

2. having the nature of an illusion; misleading; illusory
   I. elusive   A. illusive

3. singly in the designated order
   U. respectably   I. respectively   R. respectfully

4. a substance to counteract the effects of poison
   M. antidote   A. anecdote

5. to frustrate; to disconcert
   S. discomfort   E. discomfit

6. to suggest or express indirectly; to hint
   I. infer   F. imply

7. unlawful
   R. illicit   N. elicit

8. to pay out
   F. disburse   E. disperse

9. qualified; suitable
   G. eligible   T. illegible

10. lacking the means for subsistence; poor; impoverished
    T. indignant   A. indigent

__	__	L	__	__	__	__	__	__	__	__
4	10		1	9	3	7	2	6	8	5

11.2 A Submarine First

In 1958, this American submarine was the first to make an undersea crossing of the North Pole. What was the name of this submarine?

To answer the question, complete each sentence with the correct word. Choose your answers from the words after each sentence. Write the letter of each answer in the space above its sentence number at the bottom of the page. You will need to divide the letters into words. One letter is provided.

1. My parents taught me to always treat others _____ .
   E. respectably   N. respectfully   R. respectively

2. Whenever my Uncle Jim visits, he always has an _____ to tell us.
   T. anecdote   M. antidote

3. Because of several storms, we had an _____ amount of rainfall last month.
   S. access   H. excess

4. Students with an "A" average are _____ to participate in the math contest.
   L. eligible   I. illegible

5. The day's high humidity caused great _____ for everyone at the picnic.
   A. discomfort   O. discomfit

6. Based on the climate data, scientists can _____ that the Earth is warming.
   U. infer   E. imply

7. The principal tried to _____ an explanation from the student for his behavior.
   C. illicit   T. elicit

8. The cat's arrival caused the birds to _____ .
   R. disburse   S. disperse

9. The police finally arrested the _____ burglar.
   U. illusive   E. elusive

10. John was _____ that his reservations had been mistakenly canceled.
    U. indignant   O. indigent

— — — — — — — —I — — —
7   3   9   1   5   10   2   4   6   8

Easily Confused Words, III

© Gary Robert Muschla

11.3 A First for a President

1. Tyler's handwriting is <u>not decipherable</u>.
   E. eligible   I. illegible

2. Jenna's broken ankle caused her a lot of <u>distress</u>.
   A. discomfort   T. discomfit

3. Once he got inside our attic, the squirrel was <u>difficult to catch</u>.
   I. elusive   A. illusive

4. The master criminal was involved in many <u>unlawful</u> activities.
   L. elicit   A. illicit

5. Mr. Simon often starts his class with <u>a short amusing story</u>.
   N. an antidote   T. an anecdote

6. Sam works for the theater and he granted us <u>passage</u> backstage to meet the cast.
   H. excess   T. access

7. Blowing winds <u>scatter</u> seeds in all directions.
   W. disperse   B. disburse

8. The police report seemed to <u>suggest indirectly</u> that wet roads caused the accident.
   L. imply   R. infer

9. Thomas was <u>very angry</u> that no one believed he was telling the truth.
   O. indigent   F. indignant

10. The teacher met with each student <u>singly in order</u> about the science project.
    L. respectively   O. respectfully   N. respectably

$$\underline{\hphantom{x}}\quad \underline{\hphantom{x}}\quad \underline{\hphantom{x}}\quad \underline{\hphantom{x}}\quad \underline{\hphantom{x}}\quad \underline{\hphantom{x}}\quad \underline{M}\quad \underline{\hphantom{x}}\quad \underline{\hphantom{x}}\quad \underline{\hphantom{x}}\quad \underline{\hphantom{x}}$$
$$7\quad\ 3\quad\ 10\quad\ 8\quad\ 1\quad\ 4\qquad\ 5\quad\ 2\quad\ 9\quad\ 6$$

Words with Latin Roots, I

Many English words have roots that can be traced back to ancient Latin. Some Latin roots (with their meanings in parentheses) are *doc* (teach), *pater*, *patr* (father), *rupt* (break), *trib* (give), and *var* (different).

1. contribute (v): to give or supply

   I <u>contribute</u> to charity as much as possible.

2. patriarch (n): the male leader of a family or tribe

   The <u>patriarch</u> of the tribe was a wise man.

3. variety (n): the quality or condition of being diverse; an assortment

   Mom brought a <u>variety</u> of flowers to plant in the yard.

4. abrupt (adj): unexpectedly sudden; impulsive

   The <u>abrupt</u> change in the weather surprised everyone.

5. document (n): a written record; certificate; (v): to prove, certify, or validate

   A birth certificate is an official <u>document</u>.

   Erik had to <u>document</u> his sources for his history report.

6. various (adj): of diverse or different kinds; several

   There were <u>various</u> reasons for not going on vacation last year.

7. tributary (n): a stream or river that flows into a larger stream or river

   The Missouri River is the Mississippi River's main <u>tributary</u>.

8. doctrine (n): an idea; beliefs or principles; a rule

   The president announced his <u>doctrine</u> for conducting foreign policy.

9. paternal (adj): of or pertaining to a father; fatherly

   His players view Coach Smith as a <u>paternal</u> figure.

10. erupt (v): to emerge violently; explode; discharge

    We watched the volcano <u>erupt</u> on TV.

Vocabulary Tip

Words that have the same Latin roots often have related meanings.

12.1 Comets

The paths of comets around the sun are far from circular. What path do comets take around the sun?

To answer the question, match each definition on the left with its word on the right. Write the letter of each answer in the space above its definition number at the bottom of the page. You will need to divide the letters into words.

Definitions

1. male leader of a family or tribe _____

2. of diverse or different kinds; several _____

3. unexpectedly sudden; impulsive _____

4. a written record; certificate _____

5. to emerge violently; explode; discharge _____

6. a stream or river that flows into a larger stream or river _____

7. the quality or condition of being diverse; an assortment _____

8. of or pertaining to a father; fatherly _____

9. an idea; beliefs or principles; a rule _____

10. to give or supply _____

Words

R. abrupt

T. variety

E. tributary

I. doctrine

L. contribute

O. patriarch

B. paternal

P. erupt

A. document

C. various

___ ___ ___ ___ ___ ___ ___ ___ ___ ___ ___ ___ ___ ___ ___
6   10   10   9   5   7   9   2   4   10   1   3   8   9   7

12.2 King Tut

King Tut was a pharaoh (leader) of Egypt over 3,000 years ago. He was nine years old when he became pharaoh. What was King Tut's full name?

To answer the question, complete each sentence with the correct word. Choose your answers from the words that follow each sentence. Write the letter of each answer in the space above its sentence number at the bottom of the page. One letter is provided.

1. My grandfather is considered to be the _____ of our family.
   E. paternal   U. variety   A. patriarch

2. Every member of the group is expected to _____ to the project.
   R. erupt   K. contribute   N. document

3. The general stated his _____ for defending the country.
   S. document   R. tributary   N. doctrine

4. The child had a temper and was known for his _____ outbursts.
   A. abrupt   U. paternal   I. erupt

5. The students displayed a _____ of projects at the science fair.
   T. variety   L. various   S. tributary

6. We had to _____ all of our sources for our reports.
   S. abrupt   M. document   T. doctrine

7. A _____ often starts as a small stream.
   H. tributary   R. patriarch   M. contribute

8. Jim traced the _____ line of his family to his great-great grandfather.
   I. patriarch   S. tributary   E. paternal

9. The park ranger said that the geyser would _____ soon.
   A. abrupt   U. erupt   O. contribute

10. We checked a map and found _____ roads we could take to the stadium.
    M. paternal   T. various   E. variety

___ ___ ___ ___ N ___ ___ ___ ___ ___ ___
5   9   10   4   2   7   1   6   8   3

Words with Latin Roots, I

12.3 Uranus

Uranus is the only planet in our solar system that does this. What does Uranus do that no other planet in our solar system does?

To answer the question, read each sentence below. If the underlined word is used correctly, write the letter for correct in the space above its sentence number at the bottom of the page. If the underlined word is not used correctly, write the letter for incorrect. You will need to divide the letters into words. Some letters are provided.

1. Mom makes sure we have a variety of healthy snacks in our house.
   O. correct   E. incorrect

2. The old king looked upon his people in a paternal manner.
   A. correct   U. incorrect

3. The abrupt downpour caused a delay in the game.
   T. correct   M. incorrect

4. My grandmother is a patriarch of her daughters.
   C. correct   S. incorrect

5. The flower garden in our yard attracts various insects and birds.
   I. correct   E. incorrect

6. A tributary is a pond, lake, or ocean into which streams and rivers flow.
   A. correct   O. incorrect

7. The earthquake caused many old buildings to erupt and crumble.
   S. correct   E. incorrect

8. I contribute an article each month to our school's newspaper.
   N. correct   S. incorrect

9. A document is a verbal agreement between people.
   E. correct   R. incorrect

10. A doctrine is a doctor's assistant.
    N. correct   D. incorrect

$$\underline{}\ \underline{}\ \underline{T}\ \underline{}\ \underline{}\ \underline{E}\ \underline{S}\ \underline{}\ \underline{}\ \underline{}\ \underline{T}\ \underline{S}\ \underline{}\ \underline{I}\ \underline{}\ \underline{}$$

$$9\quad 6\qquad 2\quad 3\qquad\quad 1\quad 8\quad 5\qquad\quad 4\qquad 10\quad 7$$

Words with Latin Roots, II

Many English words have roots that can be traced back to ancient Latin. Some Latin roots (with their meanings in parentheses) are *alt* (high), *hosp*, *host* (guest, host), *sign* (mark), *spec* (see), and *voc* (voice).

1. insignia (n): a badge of office, membership, or rank; an emblem

   The members of the marching band wore an <u>insignia</u> on their sleeves.

2. altitude (n): the elevation of a thing above a surface

   The plane cruised at an <u>altitude</u> of several thousand feet.

3. significant (adj): meaningful; important

   Getting a driver's license is a <u>significant</u> event to most teenagers.

4. hospitable (adj): acting in a friendly and generous manner toward guests

   Whenever we visit, Aunt Janet is very <u>hospitable</u>.

5. spectacle (n): a public display or performance; something great or showy

   The clowns in the parade put on a great <u>spectacle</u>.

6. inspect (v): to examine carefully; to check

   The mayor ordered the town's engineer to <u>inspect</u> the bridge for safety.

7. advocate (ăd´ və kĭt, kāt´) (n): a person who argues for a cause; (ăd´ və kāt´) (v): to speak in favor or support of

   Tess is an <u>advocate</u> for conservation.

   I <u>advocate</u> conservation every chance I get.

8. hospital (n): an institution that provides medical care

   Richard's knee surgery was performed in a <u>hospital</u>.

9. respect (n): having regard for worth; (v): to feel or show regard for

   We should always treat other people with <u>respect</u>.

   We should always <u>respect</u> others.

10. vocal (adj): of or pertaining to the voice

    The child was very <u>vocal</u> and talked constantly.

> **Vocabulary Tip**
>
> **U**nderstanding the meaning of the roots of words can help you to understand the meanings of the words.

13.1 An Imitator

This animal is known for being able to imitate sounds. What is this animal?

To answer the question, match each definition on the left with its word on the right. Write the letter of each answer in the space above its definition number at the bottom of the page.

Definitions

Words

1. an institution that provides medical care _____

2. meaningful; important _____

3. a badge of office, membership, or rank _____

4. having regard for worth _____

5. a public display or performance _____

6. to speak in favor or support of _____

7. of or pertaining to the voice _____

8. the elevation of a thing above a surface _____

9. acting in a friendly and generous manner toward guests _____

10. to examine carefully; to check _____

O. significant

D. spectacle

I. vocal

C. inspect

G. hospital

M. altitude

K. respect

R. hospitable

N. insignia

B. advocate

___ ___ ___ ___ ___ ___ ___ ___ ___ ___ ___
8   2   10   4   7   3   1   6   7   9   5

13.2 A Barber's Son

The father of this comic strip character is a barber. Who is the character?

To answer the question, complete each sentence with the correct word. Choose your answers from the words after the sentences. Write the letter of each answer in the space above its sentence number at the bottom of the page. You will need to divide the letters into words. One letter is provided.

1. In an effort to reduce injuries, Nick's parents _____ safety in school sports.

2. Lisa's mother is a nurse who works at a _____ .

3. Cara is a _____ critic of animal abuse and often speaks out against it.

4. The halftime show at the football game was a grand _____ .

5. The math project counts as much as a test and is a _____ part of our final grade.

6. The pilot increased the plane's _____ to fly over the storm.

7. The students _____ Mrs. Sanchez for her kindness and fairness.

8. The staff at our hotel was very _____ and made our stay delightful.

9. The _____ on his sleeve indicated Alberto's rank in the conservation corps.

10. After the big storm, I helped Dad _____ the house for damage.

Answers

R. insignia   N. spectacle   C. hospitable   A. advocate   B. inspect

O. hospital   W. altitude   L. vocal   H. respect   E. significant

__	__	__	__	__	I	__	__	__	__	__	__
8	7	1	9	3		5	10	9	2	6	4

13.3 Internet Inventor

Many people consider this man to be the primary inventor of the Internet. What is his name?

To answer the question, read each sentence below. If the underlined word is used correctly, write the letter for correct in the space above its sentence number at the bottom of the page. If the underlined word is not used correctly, write the letter for incorrect. Some letters are provided.

1. Mrs. Markus is an advocate for students' rights.
   R. correct   U. incorrect

2. The play that we watched in the park was a lavish spectacle.
   S. correct   N. incorrect

3. The championship game was the most significant game of Bradley's career.
   M. correct   E. incorrect

4. Hospitable people are hardly ever welcoming.
   V. correct   N. incorrect

5. Maria is a shy, vocal student who says little in class.
   Y. correct   I. incorrect

6. People should always inspect the rights of others.
   N. correct   R. incorrect

7. Insignia is another name for a sign or billboard.
   T. correct   B. incorrect

8. When he broke his ankle, my brother had to go to the hospital.
   T. correct   J. incorrect

9. It is important that you respect yourself as well as others.
   L. correct   R. incorrect

10. The sunken ship was found at an altitude of sixty feet below the surface.
    O. correct   E. incorrect

__ __ __ __ E __ __ E __ __ - __ E __
8   5   3   7   1   4   6   2   9   10

Words with Greek Roots, I

Many English words have roots that stretch back to ancient Greece. Some Greek roots (with their meanings in parentheses) are *ast* (star), *chron* (time), *gen* (birth, race), *mech* (machine), and *soph* (wise).

1. progeny (n): children or descendants; offspring

   Colonists came to the New World so that their <u>progeny</u> would have a chance for a better life.

2. astronomy (n): the study of space and all heavenly objects

   Tony likes <u>astronomy</u> and enjoys learning about the stars and planets.

3. mechanic (n): someone skilled in using, making, or repairing machines

   The <u>mechanic</u> repaired our car.

4. chronological (adj): arranged in order according to time; sequential

   A time line is set in <u>chronological</u> order.

5. philosopher (n): a person who seeks wisdom and the truths of life

   The <u>philosopher</u> sought knowledge and understanding.

6. generate (v): to bring into existence; to produce; to create

   Power plants across the country <u>generate</u> electricity.

7. mechanism (n): a machine; a system of parts that work together like a machine

   The starting <u>mechanism</u> of the pump malfunctioned and the basement flooded.

8. chronicle (n): a record of events in the order they occurred.

   The <u>chronicle</u> told of the experiences of the early settlers.

9. asteroid (n): a rocky celestial body smaller than a typical moon

   Scientists believe that an <u>asteroid</u> crashed into the Earth and destroyed the dinosaurs.

10. sophisticated (adj): having acquired worldly knowledge; cosmopolitan; knowledgeable

    Mrs. Larsen has traveled around the world and is very <u>sophisticated</u>.

Vocabulary Tip

English words that have the same Greek roots often have related meanings.

14.1 Four Special Words

Four relatively common words in English end in *dous*. Two of them are *tremendous* and *stupendous*. What are the other two?

To answer the question, match each definition with its word. Choose your answers from the words after the definitions. Write the letter of each answer in the space above its definition number at the bottom of the page.

1. arranged in order according to time; sequential _____

2. a machine; a system of parts that work together like a machine _____

3. having acquired worldly knowledge; cosmopolitan; knowledgeable _____

4. to bring into existence; to produce; to create _____

5. children or descendants; offspring _____

6. a person who pursues wisdom and the truths of life _____

7. the scientific study of space and all heavenly objects _____

8. a record of events in the order they occurred _____

9. a rocky celestial body smaller than a typical moon _____

10. someone skilled in using, making, or repairing machines _____

Answers

Z. generate   R. philosopher   U. mechanic   H. astronomy   S. chronicle
A. mechanism   E. sophisticated   D. progeny   O. asteroid   N. chronological

__	__	__	__	__	__	__	__	__	__
7	9	6	6	3	1	5	9	10	8

__	__	__	__	__	__	__	__	__
7	2	4	2	6	5	9	10	8

14.2 A One-of-a-Kind State

Of all the states, only Maine has this. What is it?

To answer the question, complete each sentence with the correct word. Choose your answers from the words after the sentences. Write the letter of each answer in the space above its sentence number at the bottom of the page. You will need to divide the letters into words. Some letters are provided.

1. Scientists tracked an _____ that passed close by the Earth.

2. The _____ of the early colonists built a great nation.

3. Tara's grandfather uses windmills on his farm to _____ electricity.

4. Nicholas used a special _____ to remotely open the skylight.

5. For his history assignment, Mario listed the major events of the Civil War in _____ order, beginning with 1861.

6. Celeste's father works as a _____ and repairs cars.

7. A man who sought truth and wisdom, Socrates was a _____ of ancient Greece.

8. Rebecca kept a _____ of her family's journey to Oregon in 1846.

9. Mrs. Jones, our school's librarian, is very knowledgeable and _____ .

10. Alex was thrilled when he received a telescope for his birthday because he likes _____ .

Answers

B. chronological M. progeny E. philosopher H. asteroid N. mechanic
A. sophisticated S. generate W. chronicle L. astronomy T. mechanism

__	__	__	__	__	__	I	__	__
9	6	9	2	7	8		4	1

O	__	__	__	Y	__	__	__	__	__
	6	7	3		10	10	9	5	10	7

14.3 Volcano

The word *volcano* originally came from the name Vulcan. Who was Vulcan?

To answer the question, read each sentence below. Replace the underlined word or phrase with the word that has a similar meaning. Choose your answers from the words after the sentences. Write the letter of each answer in the space above its sentence number at the bottom of the page. You will need to divide the letters into words.

1. Jamaal's father is a <u>person skilled in repairing machines</u>.

2. Laurie read a <u>day-by-day account</u> of a man's journey around the world.

3. Our group had to <u>produce</u> several ideas before we chose one for our project.

4. Lila's aunt works in New York City and is very <u>knowledgeable and cosmopolitan</u>.

5. All parents hope that their <u>children</u> will enjoy a high standard of living.

6. Darius included a <u>sequential</u> list of explorers and their discoveries in his report.

7. To fix the grandfather clock, the repairman worked on the <u>system of parts</u> that operates the pendulum.

8. People from great distances came to speak with the <u>man known for his pursuit of wisdom and truth</u>.

9. The largest <u>rocky celestial body smaller than a typical moon</u> is Ceres.

10. The invention of the telescope was a great advance for <u>the study of space and heavenly objects</u>.

Answers

E. chronicle   F. mechanism   G. chronological   R. astronomy   A. mechanic
N. generate   D. asteroid   O. philosopher   I. sophisticated   M. progeny

___ ___ ___ ___ ___ ___ ___ ___ ___ ___ ___ ___ ___ ___
10 8   5   1   3   6   8   9   8   7   7   4   10 2

Words with Greek Roots, II

Many English words have roots that stretch back to ancient Greece. Some Greek roots (with their meanings in parentheses) are *aero* (air), *dem* (people), *onym* (name), *ortho* (straight, right), and *path* (disease, feeling).

1. sympathy (n): a feeling or expression of sorrow; compassion

   Our <u>sympathy</u> goes out to the families whose homes were damaged in the storm.

2. orthodox (adj): accepting traditional or established views or beliefs; conventional

   Mr. Taylor teaches in a private school because he disagrees with the <u>orthodox</u> views of public education.

3. demography (n): the study of the characteristics of the human population of an area

   In social studies, we are learning about the <u>demography</u> of the United States.

4. aerial (adj): of, in, or pertaining to the air.

   We watched exciting <u>aerial</u> performances at the air show.

5. empathy (n): understanding of another's feelings and motives

   Mrs. Lin's <u>empathy</u> is a reason she is an excellent guidance counselor.

6. pseudonym (n): a fictitious name used by an author; pen name

   Mark Twain was the <u>pseudonym</u> of Samuel Clemens.

7. epidemic (n): an outbreak of a contagious disease that spreads quickly; (adj): spreading quickly by infection; widespread

   The country suffered a flu <u>epidemic</u> last year.

   The flu was <u>epidemic</u> last year.

8. democracy (n): a form of government by the people either directly or through elected representatives

   The United States is a <u>democracy</u> in which the people elect their leaders.

9. orthodontist (n): a dentist who specializes in correcting abnormally aligned teeth

   Emily went to the <u>orthodontist</u> to get her braces.

10. anonymous (adj): having or bearing no name; of unknown authorship; unnamed

    The <u>anonymous</u> essay criticized the government.

Vocabulary Tip

Understanding Greek roots is a key to understanding the meanings of many words we use today.

15.1 Canada

The name *Canada* is derived from an Iroquoian term. What did *Canada* originally mean?

To answer the question, match each definition with its word. Choose your
answers from the words after each definition. Write the letter of each answer
in the space above its definition number at the bottom of the page.

1. a form of government by the people either directly or through elected
   representatives _____
   E. sympathy   H. demography   L. democracy

2. of, in, or pertaining to the air _____
   O. epidemic   T. aerial   S. orthodox

3. having or bearing no name; of unknown authorship; unnamed _____
   S. aerial   M. anonymous   N. pseudonym

4. a dentist who specializes in correcting abnormally aligned teeth _____
   N. orthodontist   I. empathy   E. orthodox

5. a feeling or expression of sorrow; compassion _____
   A. empathy   E. sympathy   R. demography

6. accepting traditional or established views or beliefs; conventional _____
   U. sympathy   D. pseudonym   E. orthodox

7. an outbreak of a contagious disease that spreads quickly _____
   T. epidemic   E. aerial   M. empathy

8. a fictitious name used by an author; pen name _____
   R. anonymous   U. demography   E. pseudonym

9. understanding of another's feelings and motives _____
   T. sympathy   S. empathy   W. aerial

10. the study of the characteristics of the human population of an area _____
    T. demography   C. democracy   N. sympathy

___   ___   ___   ___   ___   ___   ___   ___   ___   ___
 9   5   7   10   1   8   3   6   4   2

15.2 A Story for All Ages

In the story "Snow White and the Seven Dwarfs," the names of five of the dwarfs are Happy, Grumpy, Sneezy, Sleepy, and Dopey. What are the names of the other two?

To answer the question, complete each sentence with the correct word. Choose your answers from the words after the sentences. Write the letter of each answer in the space above its sentence number at the bottom of the page. You will need to divide the letters into words. One letter is provided.

1. In a _____, the people control their government either directly or by electing their leaders.

2. The author did not use his real name and wrote his stories under a _____ .

3. Before modern medicine, an _____ could sicken millions of people.

4. On our vacation, we flew in a helicopter for an _____ view of New York City.

5. A person who lacks _____ often has trouble understanding others' feelings.

6. The _____ caller gave the police the tip they needed to catch the thief.

7. Jason decided to become an _____ to help people whose teeth are not straight.

8. _____ is the study of the characteristics of the people of an area.

9. Madison comes from an average family and has _____ opinions on most things.

10. Megan felt _____ for her brother who sprained his ankle.

Answers

L. democracy	B. orthodox	U. epidemic	A. orthodontist	C. empathy
F. anonymous	S. aerial	O. sympathy	D. demography	H. pseudonym

__	__	__	__	__	__	__	__	N	__	__	__	__
9	7	4	2	6	3	1	7		8	8	10	5

15.3 Dolly the Sheep

In 1996, Dolly the sheep became the first of these. What did Dolly become?

To answer the question, read each sentence below. If the underlined word is used correctly, write the letter for correct in the space above its sentence number at the bottom of the page. If the underlined word is not used correctly, write the letter for incorrect. You will need to divide the letters into words. Some letters are provided.

1. Lucas offered his empathy when he heard about Tonya's misfortune.
   O. correct   E. incorrect

2. Mike has an appointment next week with his orthodox.
   A. correct   M. incorrect

3. Demography is a synonym for geography.
   E. correct   O. incorrect

4. The satellite provided detailed aerial images of the eroding coastline.
   L. correct   S. incorrect

5. The author preferred using a pseudonym instead of her real name.
   L. correct   H. incorrect

6. Democracy is a form of government in which the people can elect their leaders.
   M. correct   T. incorrect

7. The epidemic infected a small number of people, who were not contagious.
   E. correct   N. incorrect

8. The anonymous artist signed his name to all of his pictures.
   P. correct   C. incorrect

9. Kyle's orthodontist tightened his braces.
   A. correct   I. incorrect

10. Friends and family offered their sympathy to Mrs. Cooper for the loss of her husband.
    M. correct   V. incorrect

___ ___ ___ ___ ___   _D_ ___ _A_   ___ ___ ___ ___
 8   5   3   7   1   2   6   10   9   4

Words with Greek Roots, II

Prefixes, I

A prefix is a word part placed at the beginning of a word that changes the word's meaning. Following are common prefixes and their meanings.

after—after   im—not   in—not   inter—among, between   over—too much

1. improper (adj): not suited to needs or circumstances; inappropriate

   Some students displayed improper behavior during the assembly.

2. international (adj): of, relating to, or involving two or more nations; worldwide

   International cooperation is needed to address the problem of global warming.

3. overbearing (adj): overwhelming in power or importance; arrogant; bossy

   Because of his overbearing personality, Jon usually gets his way.

4. impassable (adj): that which cannot be traveled over or through; blocked; impenetrable

   The snow-covered roads were impassable.

5. interstellar (adj): between or among the stars

   Interstellar space flight is not yet possible.

6. inaudible (adj): incapable of being heard

   The message over the loudspeaker was inaudible because of static.

7. aftereffect (n): an effect following a cause after a delay; a delayed result

   The cleanup that lasted for days was an aftereffect of the hurricane.

8. overdue (adj): expected or required but not come; late

   Delivery of the sweater Chloe ordered online was overdue.

9. indecision (n): the inability or reluctance to make up one's mind; hesitation

   Billy's indecision about auditioning for the school play cost him the lead role.

10. interact (v): to act on each other

    Oxygen and carbon interact to form many compounds.

> ### Vocabulary Tip
>
> **P**refixes are added in front of a root or base word.

16.1 First for a Postage Stamp

In 1902, this president's wife was the first American woman to be pictured on a U.S. postage stamp. Who was she?

To answer the question, match each definition with its word. Choose your answers from the words after the definitions. Write the letter of each answer in the space above its definition number at the bottom of the page. You will need to divide the letters into words. Some letters are provided.

1. between or among the stars _____

2. an effect that follows a cause after a delay; a delayed result _____

3. expected or required but not come; late _____

4. that which cannot be traveled over or through; blocked; impenetrable _____

5. incapable of being heard _____

6. not suited to needs or circumstances; inappropriate _____

7. overwhelming in power or importance; arrogant; bossy _____

8. of, relating to, or involving two or more nations; worldwide _____

9. to act on each other _____

10. the inability or reluctance to make up one's mind; hesitation _____

Answers

T. overbearing	H. interact	W. indecision	S. aftereffect	M. international
I. overdue	G. inaudible	R. interstellar	A. improper	O. impassable

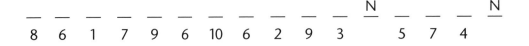

$$\underline{}\ \underline{}\ \underline{}\ \underline{}\ \underline{}\ \underline{}\ \underline{}\ \underline{}\ \underline{}\ \underline{}\ \underline{\text{N}}\ \underline{}\ \underline{}\ \underline{}\ \underline{\text{N}}$$

8 6 1 7 9 6 10 6 2 9 3   5 7 4

16.2 Penguins

Penguins are unique among birds. What do penguins do and not do that makes them different from other birds?

To answer the question, complete each sentence with the correct word. Choose your answers from the words after the sentences. Write the letter of each answer in the space above its sentence number at the bottom of the page. You will need to divide the letters into words. Some letters are provided.

1. Coming a few days later, the headaches were an _____ of the accident.

2. The mountains seemed to be an _____ barrier, blocking the way west.

3. Talking when others are speaking is _____ conduct.

4. Ann forgot to return her library book and received an e-mail that it was _____.

5. In science fiction, _____ travel is common.

6. Due to a defect on the DVD, the sound of the movie was _____.

7. Nan smiled as she watched the kitten and puppy _____ for the first time.

8. Mr. Hendricks is an arrogant, _____ person who thinks he is always right.

9. _____ on the parts of the mayor and the town council resulted in the new youth center not being built.

10. The _____ conference on energy attracted scientists from around the world.

Answers

T. improper   F. international   B. overbearing   I. impassable   M. inaudible
Y. overdue   N. aftereffect   W. indecision   S. interact   L. interstellar

$\frac{\quad}{7}$ $\frac{\quad}{9}$ $\frac{\quad}{2}$ $\frac{\quad}{6}$ $\frac{\quad}{8}$ $\frac{U}{3}$ $\frac{\quad}{1}$ $\frac{O}{3}$ $\frac{\quad}{10}$ $\frac{\quad}{5}$ $\frac{\quad}{4}$

16.3 Great Seal of the United States

The Great Seal is a symbol of the United States. The center of the Great Seal is the bald eagle, our national bird. In one claw the eagle holds arrows as a symbol for war. In the other claw he holds a symbol for peace. What is this symbol?

To answer the question, read each sentence below. Replace each underlined word or phrase with the word that has a similar meaning. Choose your answers from the words after the sentences. Write the letter of each answer in the space above its sentence number at the bottom of the page. You will need to divide the letters into words. One letter is provided.

1. In the distant future, star-to-star journeys by humans may become a reality.

2. The students acted in an inappropriate manner on the school bus.

3. Because of all the noise in the background, Daryl's phone message was impossible to hear.

4. In a science experiment, students learned that mixtures are composed of substances that do not chemically act upon each other.

5. The delayed result of last year's forest fire was the growth of new seedlings.

6. Few people are as bossy as Mrs. Jones.

7. The earthquake made several roads impossible to travel over.

8. Bekka's hesitation over the dress she wanted for the party promised a long day of shopping.

9. The multination agreement would lead to improved trade.

10. Because of bad weather, all incoming flights were late.

Answers

I. improper   L. indecision   H. aftereffect   V. overdue   N. inaudible

C. impassable   B. interact   E. interstellar   O. overbearing   R. international

<pre>
__ __ __ __ __ __ __   A   __ __ __
 6   8   2 10   1   4   9   3   7   5
</pre>

Prefixes, II

A prefix is a word part placed at the beginning of a word that changes the word's meaning. Following are common prefixes and their meanings.

be—make   il—not   ir—not   mal—bad   re—back

1. malfunction (n): a breakdown; a failure; (v): to fail to work or operate properly

   An equipment <u>malfunction</u> at the electric company caused a major power outage.

   A software glitch caused Rudy's computer to <u>malfunction</u>.

2. illiterate (adj): unable to read and write; untaught; unschooled

   In some countries, many people are <u>illiterate</u>.

3. belittle (v): to represent or speak of as unimportant; disparage

   A bully will often try to <u>belittle</u> others.

4. recede (v): to move back or away from; withdraw; retreat; ebb

   The flood waters are expected to <u>recede</u> after a few days.

5. besiege (v): to surround with troops; to harass as with offers or requests

   The enemy planned to <u>besiege</u> the castle.

6. irresistible (adj): impossible to resist; overpowering; overwhelming

   The <u>irresistible</u> donuts made Sam's mouth water.

7. illogical (adj): contradicting or disregarding sense; irrational

   Ignoring the size of the coming storm, Tom's decision not to leave the island was <u>illogical</u>.

8. irresponsible (adj): lacking a sense of responsibility; unreliable; undependable

   Whenever Ryan loses his temper, he acts in an <u>irresponsible</u> manner.

9. irregular (adj): lacking uniformity; occurring at unequal intervals; abnormal; uneven

   Uncle Ed takes medication to control an <u>irregular</u> heartbeat.

10. refurbish (v): to make clean or fresh again; renovate; renew

    Deena helped her father <u>refurbish</u> the old cabinet.

Vocabulary Tip

Understanding the meaning of its prefix can help you understand the meaning of a word.

17.1 Mercury

Mercury is an element. It is the only common metal that has this characteristic. What characteristic sets mercury apart from other metals?

To answer the question, match each definition with its word. Choose your answers from the words after the definitions. Write the letter of each answer in the space above its definition number at the bottom of the page. You will need to divide the letters into words. Some letters are provided.

1. contradicting or disregarding sense; irrational _____

2. to move back or away from; withdraw; retreat; ebb _____

3. impossible to resist; overpowering; overwhelming _____

4. a breakdown; a failure _____

5. to make clean or fresh again; renovate; renew _____

6. lacking a sense of responsibility; unreliable; undependable _____

7. unable to read and write; untaught; unschooled _____

8. lacking uniformity; occurring at unequal intervals; abnormal; uneven _____

9. to represent or speak of as unimportant; disparage _____

10. to surround with troops; to harass as with offers or requests _____

Answers

R. recede   A. refurbish   I. irregular   U. irresponsible   L. belittle
M. illogical   E. besiege   O. illiterate   Q. malfunction   T. irresistible

__	__	__	__	__	D	__	__
9	8	4	6	8	__	5	3

__	__	__	__	__	__	__	P	__	__	__	__	__	__	__
2	7	7	1	3	10	1	__	10	2	5	3	6	2	10

17.2 Goldfish

Bert, of *Sesame Street* fame, has three goldfish. One is named Melissa. What are the names of the other two?

To answer the question, find the word that means about the same as each word below. Choose your answers from the choices after each word. Write the letter of each answer in the space above its word's number at the bottom of the page. You will need to divide the letters into words. Some letters are provided.

1. belittle: N. irrational   L. disparage   S. renovate

2. malfunction: R. harass   U. overpowering   L. breakdown

3. illogical: E. unreliable   A. withdraw   D. irrational

4. refurbish: T. renew   O. uneven   N. retreat

5. irresponsible: O. unreliable   I. unimportant   A. failure

6. irregular: E. renovate   Y. abnormal   H. ebb

7. besiege: T. senseless   N. surround   C. uneven

8. recede: M. breakdown   R. disregard   T. withdraw

9. illiterate: L. unschooled   H. overpowering   M. undependable

10. irresistible: B. overpowering   C. disparage   R. abnormal

— — — E A — — — A — — —
9 6 1   7 3 8   2 10 5 4

17.3 A Big Volcano

This volcano is the biggest on Earth. From its base under the surface of the ocean, it rises more than 50,000 feet. What is its name and where is it located?

To answer the question, complete each sentence with the correct word. Choose your answers from the words after each sentence. Write the letter of each answer in the space above its sentence number at the bottom of the page. Some letters are provided.

1. The wonderful aromas of Thanksgiving dinner were _____ .
   E. irresponsible   A. irresistible   U. illogical

2. People who are _____ cannot read and write.
   I. illogical   O. irresistible   A. illiterate

3. Paulo decided to _____ the garage and turn it into a workshop.
   A. refurbish   E. besiege   Y. recede

4. The _____ of the traffic light on Main Street caused a traffic jam.
   S. recede   N. malfunction   E. irregular

5. Advertisers _____ us with junk mail.
   M. belittle   L. besiege   S. refurbish

6. As soon as the time of high tide passes, the water begins to _____.
   U. malfunction   E. belittle   I. recede

7. The Saturday meeting of the city council was highly _____ .
   H. irregular   P. illiterate   C. refurbish

8. The teacher explained to Robbie how his recent behavior was _____.
   R. malfunction   O. illiterate   M. irresponsible

9. Jonathan's answer to the essay was _____ because he ignored important facts.
   T. irregular   K. illiterate   W. illogical

10. Tina was taught to always respect others and never _____ anyone.
    I. belittle   N. recede   E. malfunction

```
__  __  U   __  A    __  O  __ ,  __  A  __  __  __  __
8   2   4       5    1       7      9   3  10   6
```

© Gary Robert Muschla

68

Suffixes, I

A suffix is a word part placed at the end of a word. Suffixes add to the meaning of words to which they are added. Following are some common suffixes.

an—relating to   ance—state or quality of   ary, ory—place for
ious—state or quality of   ous—full of

1. **nervous** (adj): easily excited; high-strung; apprehensive

   No matter how much she studies, Carrie is always <u>nervous</u> before tests.

2. **annoyance** (n): something that bothers; irritation; exasperation

   My little sister can be a huge <u>annoyance</u>, especially when I have friends over.

3. **laboratory** (n): a place equipped for conducting scientific experiments or research; lab

   Sharyn's mother is a scientist and works in a <u>laboratory</u>.

4. **ambitious** (adj): eager to achieve; purposeful

   Jasmine is <u>ambitious</u> and works hard to succeed.

5. **veteran** (n): a person who has served long in a cause or position; (adj): experienced; knowledgeable

   My grandfather is an army <u>veteran</u>.

   My aunt is a <u>veteran</u> police officer.

6. **resistance** (n): an act of opposition; defiance

   Once he was surrounded by the police, the robber offered no <u>resistance</u>.

7. **nutritious** (adj): providing nourishment; nourishing

   Mom makes sure all our meals are <u>nutritious</u>.

8. **infirmary** (n): a place for care of the sick or injured; a small hospital, especially in another building

   When my sister twisted her ankle at camp, she went to the <u>infirmary</u>.

9. **wondrous** (adj): wonderful; astonishing; marvelous; spectacular

   The rainbow curving over the valley was <u>wondrous</u>.

10. **urban** (adj): of or located in a city; characteristic of city life; metropolitan

    Khalil prefers living in an <u>urban</u> area rather than a small town.

> **Vocabulary Tip**
>
> **L**earning the meanings of suffixes can help you understand the meanings of words.

18.1 Colonial Newspaper Editor

In the early 1760s, Rhode Islander Ann Franklin became the first woman to hold the title of newspaper editor. What publication did she edit?

To answer the question, match each definition with its word. Choose your answers from the words after the definitions. Write the letter of each answer in the space above its definition number at the bottom of the page. Some letters are provided.

1. eager to achieve; purposeful _____

2. providing nourishment; nourishing _____

3. an act of opposition; defiance _____

4. easily excited; high-strung; apprehensive _____

5. of or located in a city; characteristic of city life; metropolitan _____

6. a place for care of the sick or injured; a small hospital _____

7. wonderful; astonishing; marvelous; spectacular _____

8. a person who has served long in a cause or position _____

9. something that bothers; irritation; exasperation _____

10. a place equipped for conducting scientific experiments or research _____

Answers

| W. nervous | T. wondrous | H. laboratory | M. veteran | C. urban |
| E. annoyance | P. ambitious | O. infirmary | R. resistance | Y. nutritious |

___ ___ ___ <u>N</u> ___ ___ ___ ___ ___ ___ ___ ___ ___ ___ <u>U</u> ___ ___
 7 10 9   9 4 1 6 3 7   8 9 3 5   3 2

Suffixes, I

18.2 A Crayon Milestone

The Crayola company has produced billions of crayons. What was the special name of the hundred billionth crayon made by Crayola?

To answer the question, find the word or phrase that means about the same as each word below. Choose your answers from the choices that follow each word. Write the letter of each answer in the space above its word's number at the bottom of the page. You will need to divide the letters into words.

1. resistance: E. spectacular   O. apprehensive   I. defiance

2. infirmary: S. very eager   E. high-strung   N. small hospital

3. wondrous: B. marvelous   M. defiance   R. experienced

4. laboratory: A. opposition   E. lab   I. knowledgeable

5. nutritious: O. nourishing   S. astonishing   M. irritation

6. ambitious: I. wonderful   R. purposeful   N. in a city

7. veteran: A. exasperation   Y. metropolitan   U. experienced

8. nervous: B. easily excited   V. spectacular   G. eager to achieve

9. annoyance: R. defiance   L. irritation   I. spectacular

10. urban: S. exasperation   B. metropolitan   M. astonishing

___   ___   ___   ___   ___   ___   ___   ___   ___   ___
 8   9   7   4   6   1   10   3   5   2

Suffixes, I

18.3 A Forgotten Character

Walt Disney created many famous cartoon characters, including Mickey Mouse, Donald Duck, and Goofy. What was the name of Disney's first animal cartoon star?

To answer the question, complete each sentence with the correct word. Choose your answers from the words after the sentences. Write the letter of each answer in the space above its sentence number at the bottom of the page. You will need to divide the letters into words. Some letters are provided.

1. William is an _____ boy, whose goal is to become a billionaire someday.

2. Fruits are good choices for _____ snacks.

3. The defenders stopped the enemy by mounting a strong _____.

4. Lindsay was _____ as she waited for her turn during the piano recital.

5. Being the most experienced pitcher, Roberto was the _____ of the pitching staff.

6. After moving to the city, Angela quickly settled into _____ life.

7. Lauren's mother works as a nurse in the _____ of a college.

8. The fireworks display over the river was a _____ sight.

9. Being caught in a traffic jam was another _____ in a day of many irritations.

10. Thomas Edison conducted experiments in his _____ in Menlo Park, New Jersey.

Answers

B. laboratory	O. nervous	T. wondrous	I. annoyance	C. nutritious
K. ambitious	E. veteran	L. resistance	S. infirmary	A. urban

```
__   __   W    __   __   D    __   H    __
 4    7         6    3         8         5
```

```
__   U    __   __   Y    R    __   __   __   __
 3    2    1              6    10   10   9    8
```

Suffixes, I

Suffixes, II

A suffix is a word part placed at the end of a word. Suffixes add to the meaning of words to which they are added. Following are some common suffixes.

ade—action or process ence—state or quality of ify—to make
ity, ty—state or quality of ulent—full of

1. blockade (n): the closing of a place such as a city or harbor by hostile forces; barrier; (v): to close off an area

   The <u>blockade</u> cut off the city's supplies.

   During the Civil War, the North tried to <u>blockade</u> the South's ports.

2. necessity (n): something essential; of urgent need; requirement

   Food is a <u>necessity</u> of life.

3. unity (n): the condition of being one; singleness of purpose or action; union; solidarity

   Countries around the world must work in <u>unity</u> to save the Earth's resources.

4. fraudulent (adj): deceitful; deceptive; dishonest

   The contract my grandmother signed for home repairs was <u>fraudulent</u>.

5. vilify (v): to defame; to denigrate; to slander

   Some political candidates would rather <u>vilify</u> their opponents than discuss the issues.

6. turbulent (adj): greatly agitated; stirred-up; tumultuous

   The <u>turbulent</u> river was ideal for white-water rafting.

7. violence (n): physical, damaging force; fury; intensity; fighting

   The <u>violence</u> of the tornado was indescribable.

8. amnesty (n): a general pardon granted by a government; pardon

   The government offered <u>amnesty</u> to all rebels who stopped fighting.

9. absence (n): the state of being away; nonattendance; lack; shortcoming

   Jacob's <u>absence</u> was caused by the flu.

10. terrify (v): to fill with extreme fear; to frighten; to alarm

    Thunderstorms <u>terrify</u> our dog.

Vocabulary Tip

Some suffixes change a word's part of speech. The suffix *ulent*, for example, added to the noun *fraud* makes the adjective *fraudulent*.

© Gary Robert Muschla

19.1 Play Ball!

On September 14, 1990, this father and son became the only father and son to hit back-to-back homeruns in a major league baseball game. Who are they?

To answer the question, match each definition with its word. Choose your answers from the words after the definitions. Write the letter of each answer in the space above its definition number at the bottom of the page. Some letters are provided.

1. greatly agitated; stirred-up; tumultuous _____

2. a general pardon granted by a government _____

3. to fill with extreme fear; to frighten; to alarm _____

4. the closing of a place such as a city or harbor by hostile forces; barrier _____

5. deceitful; deceptive; dishonest _____

6. to defame; to denigrate; to slander _____

7. the condition of being one; singleness of purpose or action _____

8. something essential; of urgent need; requirement _____

9. the state of being away; nonattendance; lack; shortcoming _____

10. physical, damaging force; fury; intensity; fighting _____

Answers

R. blockade   F. necessity   G. vilify   Y. amnesty   J. absence
K. fraudulent   I. turbulent   E. terrify   O. violence   N. unity

__ __ __   __ __ __ __ __ __ __'
5 3 7   6 4 1 8 8 3 2

__ U __ __ __ __   A __ D   S __ __ __ __ __
9 7 1 10 4   7   3 7 1 10 4

19.2 West of the Mississippi

Born in Iowa, this president was the first president to be born west of the Mississippi River. Who was he?

To answer the question, find the word or phrase that has a similar meaning to each word below. Choose your answers from the words or phrases after each word. Write the letter of each answer in the space above its word's number at the bottom of the page. You will need to divide the letters into words. Some letters are provided.

1. absence: A. tumultuous   H. solidarity   E. nonattendance

2. necessity: O. slander   E. requirement   N. alarm

3. vilify: R. defame   S. deceptive   A. agitated

4. amnesty: S. shortcoming   A. denigrate   V. pardon

5. turbulent: O. frighten   R. stirred-up   M. urgent need

6. blockade: D. lack   N. physical force   R. barrier

7. violence: O. fighting   I. frighten   E. dishonest

8. unity: A. damaging   H. solidarity   J. pardon

9. terrify: H. frighten   L. defame   D. union

10. fraudulent: E. requirement   A. very agitated   B. deceitful

__	__	__	__	E	__	T	__	__	O	__	__	__
8	1	5	10	3		9	7		4	2	6	

19.3 Milwaukee

Milwaukee is an Algonquian term. What is *Milwaukee* thought to have meant in Algonquian?

To answer the question, complete each sentence with the correct word. Choose your answers from the words after the sentences. Write the letter of each answer in the space above its sentence number at the bottom of the page. You will need to divide the letters into words. One letter is provided.

1. In _____, the thirteen American colonies fought the British.

2. The _____ waves crashed against the shore.

3. Janie handed her teacher the note explaining her recent _____ from school.

4. Mrs. Ellis told her students of the _____ for taking notes in class.

5. The letter contained untrue facts and was an attempt to _____ the mayor.

6. The _____ prevented anyone from entering or leaving the city.

7. The police found that the car thief had a _____ driver's license.

8. _____ should never be used to settle arguments.

9. After the civil war, the king granted _____ to all of his subjects who had fought against him.

10. Jason hoped that the horror movie would not _____ his younger brother.

Answers

R. necessity   O. violence   P. blockade   L. amnesty   S. unity

E. fraudulent   G. terrify   A. vilify   C. absence   D. turbulent

$\frac{}{5}$ $\frac{}{10}$ $\frac{}{8}$ $\frac{}{8}$ $\frac{}{2}$ $\frac{}{1}$ $\frac{}{6}$ $\frac{}{8}$ $\frac{T}{8}$ $\frac{}{4}$ $\frac{}{6}$ $\frac{}{9}$ $\frac{}{5}$ $\frac{}{3}$ $\frac{}{7}$

Words That Name, I

Nouns are words that name a person, place, thing, or idea. Without nouns, nothing would have a name.

1. banquet (n): a great feast; a formal dinner

   We attended a <u>banquet</u> honoring our town's firefighters.

2. fiasco (n): a big or humiliating failure

   Our attempt to give our dog a bath was a <u>fiasco</u>.

3. dynasty (n): a line of rulers of the same family

   A <u>dynasty</u> ruled the country for over a thousand years.

4. catastrophe (n): a great and sudden disaster; calamity; debacle

   The earthquake was a <u>catastrophe</u> for towns near the fault line.

5. perception (n): the process of becoming aware through the senses

   A good detective has keen <u>perception</u>.

6. treason (n): a person's betrayal of his or her sovereign or country; disloyalty

   Benedict Arnold committed <u>treason</u> during the Revolutionary War.

7. memorandum (n): a short note of something to be remembered; a reminder

   The <u>memorandum</u> informed the camp's staff of the Tuesday meeting.

8. expertise (n): specialized skill or knowledge

   Carla is a great overall dancer, but her <u>expertise</u> lies in ballet.

9. proprietor (n): the owner of a business

   Mr. Harris is the <u>proprietor</u> of a candy shop.

10. adversary (n): an enemy; an opponent; a foe

    For the wrestling tournament, Raymond's best friend was an <u>adversary</u>.

> **Vocabulary Tip**
>
> **T**he word *noun* comes from the Latin word *nomen*, which means "name."

20.1 An American Novelist

This man is considered by many to be the first great American novelist. Among his many novels was *The Last of the Mohicans*, *The Pathfinder*, and *The Deerslayer*. Who was he?

To answer the question, match each definition with its word. Choose your answers from the words after the definitions. Write the letter of each answer in the space above its definition number at the bottom of the page. Some letters are provided.

1. a big or humiliating failure _____

2. a short note of something to be remembered _____

3. the owner of a business _____

4. an enemy; an opponent; a foe _____

5. the process of becoming aware through the senses _____

6. specialized skill or knowledge _____

7. a great and sudden disaster; calamity; debacle _____

8. a person's betrayal of his or her sovereign or country; disloyalty _____

9. a line of rulers of the same family _____

10. a great feast; a formal dinner _____

Answers

R. memorandum   S. perception   J. catastrophe   N. fiasco   E. banquet
C. dynasty   A. adversary   O. expertise   F. treason   M. proprietor

<u> </u> <u> </u> <u> </u> <u> </u> <u> </u>   <u> </u> <u> </u> <u> </u> <u>I</u> <u> </u> <u> </u> <u> </u> <u> </u>
7   4   3   10   5   8   10   1   3   6   2   10

<u> </u> <u> </u> <u> </u> <u>P</u> <u> </u> <u> </u>
9   6   6   10   2

20.2 Under the Sea

This reinforced spherical chamber is designed to dive deep below the surface of the ocean. What is it called?

To answer the question, complete each sentence with the correct word. Choose your answers from the words after each sentence. Write the letter of each answer in the space above its sentence number at the bottom of the page. One letter is provided.

1. Jimmie uses his _____ in electronics to fix computers.
   N. dynasty   S. proprietor   E. expertise

2. The long drought proved to be a _____ for farmers.
   A. catastrophe   E. banquet   O. memorandum

3. Lucy's mom is the _____ of the dance studio on Main Street.
   M. perception   Y. proprietor   R. dynasty

4. The criminal Joker is superhero Batman's _____.
   S. treason   H. adversary   W. proprietor

5. Traci did not receive the _____ and missed the meeting.
   R. memorandum   E. expertise   O. adversary

6. The _____ was held in a downtown restaurant.
   N. memorandum H. banquet   R. dynasty

7. _____ is a serious offense, punishable by long imprisonment or death.
   L. Fiasco   U. Expertise   T. Treason

8. A person's _____ relies on her ability to see, hear, smell, taste, and touch.
   E. perception   U. catastrophe   A. memorandum

9. Because of the heavy rain, our family picnic turned into a _____.
   H. banquet   B. fiasco   S. proprietor

10. With the overthrow of the king, the _____ was ended.
    T. treason   W. adversary   S. dynasty

__	__	__	__	__	__	P	__	__	__	__
9	2	7	4	3	10		6	8	5	1

Words That Name, I

20.3 An Unusual Snake

The anaconda is one of the world's largest snakes. Aside from its size, what makes the anaconda different from most other snakes?

To answer the question, read each sentence below. Replace each underlined word or phrase with the word that has a similar meaning. Choose your answers from the words after the sentences. Write the letter of each answer in the space above its sentence number at the bottom of the page. Some letters are provided.

1. The kingdom was ruled by the <u>members of the same family</u> for generations.

2. The smart mouse views the cat as an <u>enemy</u>.

3. Callie's father is the <u>owner</u> of a service station.

4. To a toddler, carelessly breaking her favorite toy is a <u>calamity</u>.

5. The athletic department sponsored a <u>formal dinner</u> to honor the school's all-stars.

6. After his <u>betrayal of the king</u> was discovered, the duke fled the country.

7. The <u>short reminder</u> of the day of the class trip was sent to all teachers.

8. The bodyguard relied on his sharp <u>senses and awareness</u> to protect the celebrity.

9. Jason's <u>specialized skill</u> in piano tuning is remarkable.

10. Trying to glue the pieces of the broken vase back together was a <u>big failure</u>.

Answers

O. adversary   R. banquet   G. treason   N. fiasco   E. memorandum
Y. catastrophe   V. perception   L. dynasty   B. expertise   S. proprietor

__	__	A	__	__		__	I	__	__		__	__	U	__	__
9	7		5	3		1		8	7		4	2		10	6

Words That Name, II

Nouns are words that name a person, place, thing, or idea. Without nouns, nothing would have a name.

1. plumage (n): the feathers of a bird

   Male peacocks are known for their magnificent <u>plumage</u>.

2. legacy (n): something handed down or bequeathed by a predecessor; estate

   The greatest part of my grandfather's <u>legacy</u> was his wonderful collection of books.

3. ingredient (n): a substance that is in a mixture or compound; component; part

   Sugar was a major <u>ingredient</u> of the cake Alana baked.

4. posterity (n): future generations

   Our current generation should leave a cleaner Earth for <u>posterity</u>.

5. lobbyist (n): a person who attempts to influence lawmakers on behalf of special interest groups

   The <u>lobbyist</u> urged the senator to support laws that would encourage conservation.

6. plague (n): a highly infectious disease; a pestilence

   During the Middle Ages, a <u>plague</u> killed millions of people.

7. clarity (n): the state of being clear; lucidity; distinctiveness

   Everyone understood Roger's ideas because he explained them with great <u>clarity</u>.

8. interpreter (n): a person who translates one language into another

   Camille's aunt works at the United Nations as an <u>interpreter</u>.

9. aviary (n): a large enclosure for keeping birds

   The zoo we visited had an <u>aviary</u>.

10. sage (n): a person known for his or her wisdom and judgment; philosopher; intellectual

    Before making important decisions, the village chief sought the advice of the <u>sage</u>.

> **Vocabulary Tip**
>
> **I**n English sentences, nouns can serve as the subject of a sentence, the object of a verb, the object of a preposition, a predicate noun, or as an appositive.

21.1 A Famous Rabbit

Bugs Bunny, who first appeared in cartoons in the early 1940s, was not a completely original character. He evolved from an earlier cartoon character who appeared in the mid-1930s. Who was this character?

To answer the question, match each word with its definition. Choose your answers from the words after each definition. Write the letter of each answer in the space above its definition number at the bottom of the page. You will need to divide the letters into words. One letter is provided.

1. a person who translates one language into another _____
   A. interpreter   S. clarity   M. lobbyist

2. a person who attempts to influence lawmakers on behalf of special interest groups _____
   N. sage   P. lobbyist   R. aviary

3. the feathers of a bird _____
   T. plumage   D. posterity   S. aviary

4. a person known for his or her wisdom and judgment _____
   U. interpreter   I. legacy   Y. sage

5. a substance that is in a mixture or compound; component; part _____
   W. clarity   R. ingredient   H. plague

6. a large enclosure for keeping birds _____
   E. legacy   I. aviary   A. plumage

7. the state or quality of being clear; lucidity; distinctiveness _____
   P. clarity   M. legacy   S. interpreter

8. future generations _____
   N. legacy   T. lobbyist   B. posterity

9. something handed down or bequeathed by a predecessor; estate _____
   M. posterity   H. legacy   R. aviary

10. a highly infectious disease; a pestilence _____
    G. plumage   E. posterity   B. plague

___ ___ ___ ___ ___ ___   A   ___ ___ ___ ___
 9   1   7   2   4   5   10   8   6   3

21.2 Cracker Jack

People have been enjoying Cracker Jacks as a tasty snack for over a hundred years. What are the names of the boy and dog on the Cracker Jack box?

To answer the question, complete each sentence with the correct word. Choose your answers from the words after the sentences. Write the letter of each answer in the space above its sentence number at the bottom of the page. You will need to divide the letters into words. Some letters are provided.

1. The old man was a _____, respected for his intelligence and reason.

2. Some scientists worry that a modern-day _____ could kill countless people.

3. An _____ must be accurate when translating one language into another.

4. The _____ of some birds, such as cardinals and blue jays, is distinctive.

5. The company hired a _____ in hopes of influencing members of Congress to pass certain laws.

6. With sharp _____, the president outlined his plan for the nation.

7. Because of damage from the storm, some birds escaped from the _____.

8. The Constitution was written for the people of the time and also for _____.

9. Mr. Harper's _____ to his family was the successful company he had founded.

10. Maria checked the cookie recipe to make sure she had the right amount of each _____.

Answers

J. interpreter   I. legacy   C. clarity   N. plumage   G. posterity

A. ingredient   D. sage   O. aviary   S. lobbyist   L. plague

__ __ __ __ R __ __ __ K __ __ __ B __ __ __ __
5 10 9 2 7   3 10 6   10 4 1   9 4 8 7

Words That Name, II

21.3 Breaking the Sound Barrier

In 1947, Chuck Yeager became the first man to fly faster than the speed of sound. In 1953, the first woman flew faster than the speed of sound. Who was she?

To answer the question, read each sentence below. If the underlined word is used correctly, write the letter for correct in the space above its sentence number at the bottom of the page. If the underlined word is not used correctly, write the letter for incorrect. Some letters are provided.

1. An <u>interpreter</u> is a person to whom others go for advice.
   E. correct   U. incorrect

2. We learned that the <u>aviary</u> contains more than a hundred species of fish.
   M. correct   H. incorrect

3. The adults living in our country now are our <u>posterity</u>.
   E. correct   J. incorrect

4. Seeking knowledge, people journeyed miles to speak with the <u>sage</u>.
   I. correct   O. incorrect

5. Many people were cured because of the <u>plague</u>.
   M. correct   R. incorrect

6. In a sudden burst of <u>clarity</u>, Nathan realized the answer to the problem.
   A. correct   I. incorrect

7. The <u>plumage</u> of polar bears is white.
   S. correct   Q. incorrect

8. Marissa knew that adding one wrong <u>ingredient</u> could ruin the pie.
   E. correct   N. incorrect

9. The <u>lobbyist</u> hoped to meet with members of Congress.
   C. correct   K. incorrect

10. Mrs. Thompson's <u>legacy</u> was a new park for everyone to enjoy.
    N. correct   E. incorrect

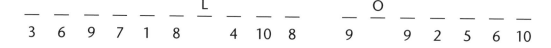

__ __ __ __ L __ __ __ __ O __ __ __ __ __
3 6 9 7 1 8   4 10 8   9   9 2 5 6 10

Words That Name, II

Words That Name, III

Nouns are words that name a person, place, thing, or idea. Without nouns, nothing would have a name.

1. chauffeur (n): a person employed to drive a car

   Mark is a <u>chauffeur</u> and works for Mr. Reynolds.

2. facade (n): the face of a building; a false appearance

   The building's brick <u>facade</u> had begun to crack.

3. artifact (n): an object produced by a human being

   The most valuable <u>artifact</u> found at the ancient village was an undamaged clay pot.

4. kindred (n): a group of people related by blood; a person's relatives; kinfolk

   Tara's <u>kindred</u> all come from Ireland.

5. amateur (n): a person who does something without professional skill; a novice

   Tess is a wonderful dancer but she still considers herself to be an <u>amateur</u>.

6. apparition (n): a ghostly figure; a specter

   Kelli was certain she saw an <u>apparition</u> in the window of the old house.

7. entrepreneur (n): a person who starts a business

   When Karl started his lawn service, he became an <u>entrepreneur</u>.

8. applicant (n): a person who applies for a position

   Chelsey was the most qualified <u>applicant</u> for the job.

9. inhabitant (n): a permanent resident of a place

   The tall stranger was an <u>inhabitant</u> of the distant valley.

10. anthropologist (n): a scientist who studies the origins and development of human beings

    Trisha's father is an <u>anthropologist</u> at the museum.

> **Vocabulary Tip**
>
> **N**ouns may be singular or plural. Most plural forms of English nouns have an -s or -es ending. Irregular nouns have various endings or no ending at all.

22.1 Minnesota

The name *Minnesota* comes from a word of the Native American Dakota tribe. What did *Minnesota* originally mean?

To answer the question, match each definition with its word. Choose your answers from the words after the definitions. Write the letter of each answer in the space above its definition number at the bottom of the page. You will need to divide the letters into words. One letter is provided.

1. a permanent resident of a place _____

2. a person who applies for a position _____

3. a group of people related by blood; a person's relatives; kinfolk _____

4. a person who starts a business _____

5. a person who does something without professional skill _____

6. a ghostly figure; a specter _____

7. a person employed to drive a car _____

8. an object produced by a human being _____

9. the face of a building; a false appearance _____

10. a scientist who studies the origins and development of human beings _____

Answers

K. chauffeur   W. anthropologist   I. artifact   A. kindred   D. inhabitant
S. applicant   E. entrepreneur   Y. amateur   T. facade   R. apparition

__	__	__	-	__	__	N	__	__	__	__	__	__	__	__
2	7	5		9	8		9	4	1	10	3	9	4	6

22.2 King Kong

In the movie *King Kong*, the great ape climbed a well-known building in New York City. What is the name of this building?

To answer the question, complete each sentence with the correct word. Choose your answers from the words after each sentence. Write the letter of each answer in the space above its sentence number at the bottom of the page. You will need to divide the letters into words. Some letters are provided.

1. Jonathan was the best _____ for the position of assistant manager.
   E. apparition   N. chauffeur   T. applicant

2. Natalie and her _____ all live in Kentucky.
   M. kindred   H. facade   R. amateur

3. Emily has been an _____ of the city all her life.
   E. inhabitant   Y. entrepreneur   S. apparition

4. James works as a _____ driving people to and from the airport.
   A. facade   E. chauffeur   U. kindred

5. Melanie's ghost costume was so detailed that she looked like a real _____.
   O. entrepreneur   I. artifact   H. apparition

6. Evan is an _____ boxer who hopes to be a professional someday.
   M. applicant   L. inhabitant   S. amateur

7. The _____ of the ancient tomb was made of massive stones.
   C. artifact   T. facade   R. apparition

8. Mr. Jones is an _____ who started several businesses over the years.
   R. entrepreneur   M. applicant   V. anthropologist

9. Tess wants to be an _____ and study the origins of humans.
   E. inhabitant   A. anthropologist   O. amateur

10. The _____ clearly came from a prehistoric settlement.
    U. amateur   P. artifact   R. applicant

__ __ __ E __ __ I __ E __ T __ __ __ (Building)
7 5 4   2 10   8   6   9 1 3

22.3 A Very Loud Animal

This sea creature is considered to be the loudest animal on Earth. Its call, which can reach levels of up to 188 decibels, can be heard for hundreds of miles underwater. What animal is this?

To answer the question, read each sentence below. If the underlined word is used correctly, write the letter for correct in the space above its sentence number at the bottom of the page. If the underlined word is not used correctly, write the letter for incorrect. You will need to divide the letters into words.

1. In his or her work to study space, an anthropologist uses a telescope.
   U. correct   E. incorrect

2. A chauffeur should be an experienced driver.
   E. correct   S. incorrect

3. David is an entrepreneur who founded a company that recycles old computers.
   A. correct   T. incorrect

4. The lighthouse keeper was the only inhabitant of the small island.
   A. correct   O. incorrect

5. The artifact was a jawbone of a dinosaur.
   H. correct   B. incorrect

6. Todd admired the facade in the basement of the building
   R. correct   H. incorrect

7. The apparition appeared at the top of the stairs and slowly floated downward.
   U. correct   Y. incorrect

8. Someone's kindred includes all of the people she knows.
   T. correct   L. incorrect

9. Every applicant for the job was required to answer questions about her experience.
   W. correct   N. incorrect

10. An amateur is a young professional.
    D. correct   L. incorrect

___ ___ ___ ___ ___ ___ ___ ___ ___ ___
3   5   10   7   1   9   6   4   8   2

Words That Name, IV

Nouns are words that name a person, place, thing, or idea. Without nouns, nothing would have a name.

1. braggart (n): a person who boasts; a boaster

   Alec is a <u>braggart</u> who tells everyone about all the great things he has done.

2. perjury (n): the willful giving of false testimony while under oath

   By lying when he was on the witness stand, the man committed <u>perjury</u>.

3. evidence (n): that which seems to prove or disprove something; proof

   The jury considered the <u>evidence</u> carefully before reaching a decision.

4. tenet (n): an opinion or principle that a person or organization believes to be true

   A <u>tenet</u> of our school's conservation club is that individuals have a responsibility to conserve the Earth's resources.

5. stalemate (n): a situation in which further action by opponents is impossible; deadlock

   Marty and I reached a <u>stalemate</u> in our chess game.

6. agenda (n): a list of things to be done, especially for a meeting; a schedule

   The <u>agenda</u> for the staff meeting was two pages long.

7. premonition (n): a warning in advance; a forewarning

   Despite the forecast of nice weather, Marlena took her umbrella because she had a <u>premonition</u> it would rain.

8. controversy (n): a dispute between sides holding different opinions; a quarrel

   The <u>controversy</u> over whether to build a new high school divided the townspeople.

9. acquaintance (n): a person someone knows; knowledge of a person or thing

   Matt is an <u>acquaintance</u> of mine.

10. enigma (n): a thing that puzzles or baffles; a puzzle; a mystery

    How our dog kept getting out of our fenced-in yard was an <u>enigma</u>.

Vocabulary Tip

A complete sentence requires two words: a noun and a verb.

23.1 An Archenemy

This man is the archenemy of famed detective Sherlock Holmes. Who is he?

To answer the question, match each definition with its word. Choose your answers from the words after the definitions. Write the letter of each answer in the space above its definition number at the bottom of the page. One letter is provided.

1. a dispute between sides holding different opinions; a quarrel _____

2. an opinion or principle that a person or organization believes to be true _____

3. a person someone knows; knowledge of a person or thing _____

4. a thing that puzzles or baffles; a puzzle; a mystery _____

5. a person who boasts; a boaster _____

6. a situation in which further action by opponents is impossible; a deadlock _____

7. a list of things to be done, especially for a meeting; a schedule _____

8. that which can prove or disprove something; proof _____

9. a warning in advance; a forewarning _____

10. the willful giving of false testimony while under oath _____

Answers

T. tenet	S. agenda	M. evidence	F. braggart	O. acquaintance
R. perjury	Y. enigma	E. controversy	I. stalemate	P. premonition

— — — — — — — — —   — — — — A — — —
9 10 3 5 1 7 7 3 10   8 3 10 6   10 2 4

23.2 Alabama

The name *Alabama* comes from a Choctaw word. What did *Alabama* originally mean?

To answer the question, complete each sentence with the correct word. Choose your answers from the words after the sentences. Write the letter of each answer in the space above its sentence number at the bottom of the page.

1. Plans for celebrating Earth Day were listed on the _____ for the teacher's meeting.

2. The odd sounds that came from the swamp every Halloween were an _____.

3. Kayla had an awful _____ that she should not take the bus to work.

4. A friend is more than an _____.

5. The idea for students to wear uniforms at our school is a _____, with some people for it and some against it.

6. The _____ boasted of all his accomplishments.

7. With neither side willing to compromise, the negotiations came to a _____.

8. While under oath, the defendant gave false information and was guilty of _____.

9. The main _____ of the charity is that no one in need is turned away.

10. The police had _____ linking the accused thief to the burglary.

Answers

E. evidence   S. controversy   L. premonition   H. braggart   A. enigma

C. stalemate   R. perjury   I. acquaintance   K. agenda   T. tenet

__ __ __ __ __ __ __ - __ __ __ __ __ __ __ __

9   6   4   7   1   10   9   7   3   10   2   8   10   8   5

23.3 A Chicago First

In 1893, Chicago became the first city in the United States to have this. What was it?

To answer the question, read each sentence below. Replace the underlined word or phrase with the word or phrase that has a similar meaning. Choose your answers from the words or phrases after each sentence. Write the letter of each answer in the space above its sentence number at the bottom of the page. You will need to divide the letters into words.

1. Willfully giving false testimony while under oath is a serious offense.
   E. An agenda   U. Perjury   O. An enigma

2. The dispute over whether to change the school lunch menu involved most of the students.
   I. tenet   S. evidence   A. controversy

3. It was a mystery how the bumbling detective always solved his cases.
   I. an enigma   E. a premonition   N. perjury

4. While shopping at the mall, Vanessa saw a person she knew from work.
   A. an acquaintance   O. an enigma   I. a stalemate

5. Jan sent the list of things to be done for the meeting to the club's members.
   A. agenda   U. controversy   Y. evidence

6. Rhonda is a boaster and always tells us about her wonderful vacations.
   S. tenet   C. stalemate   N. braggart

7. The long skid marks were proof that the car was speeding before the accident.
   A. an enigma   U. evidence   E. a tenet

8. We played several tick-tack-toe games to a deadlock.
   O. controversy   R. stalemate   N. perjury

9. The forewarning that something bad would soon happen made Luis shudder.
   M. premonition   S. tenet   N. enigma

10. Mr. Gonzales runs his business according to a simple principle: give the customer the best service possible.
    M. acquaintance   R. enigma   Q. tenet

___ ___ ___ ___ ___ ___ ___ ___ ___ ___
 2   6   4   10   1   5   8   3   7   9

Action Words, I

English words that express action are a major category of verbs. They add strength and vigor to speaking and writing.

1. **conserve** (v): to protect from loss; to use carefully; to avoid waste; to save; to preserve

   Everyone should try to <u>conserve</u> energy.

2. **determine** (v): to decide or settle, for example, a question or argument; to find out; to resolve

   Scientists could not <u>determine</u> the exact course the falling satellite would take.

3. **amplify** (v): to make larger or more powerful; to increase; to enlarge

   The magic potion will <u>amplify</u> the evil wizard's power.

4. **encompass** (v): to form a circle or ring around; to surround; to enclose

   The enemy's plan was to <u>encompass</u> the fort.

5. **accommodate** (v): to do a service or favor for; to oblige; to assist

   The staff at the hotel try to <u>accommodate</u> every guest.

6. **capitulate** (v): to surrender; to give in

   The commander of the fort refused to <u>capitulate</u>.

7. **contemplate** (v): to look at thoughtfully; to consider; to ponder

   Every high school student is wise to <u>contemplate</u> his or her future.

8. **ratify** (v): to give sanction to; to confirm; to approve

   The council members voted to <u>ratify</u> the new recycling schedule for the town.

9. **prescribe** (v): to set down as a rule or direction to be followed; to order, especially the use of a medicine; to direct

   After checking Jillian's sore throat, the doctor decided to <u>prescribe</u> an antibiotic.

10. **prevail** (v): to gain mastery over; to be greater in strength or influence; to triumph

    The king told his subjects that they must <u>prevail</u> against the invaders.

> **Vocabulary Tip**
>
> **M**ost English verbs express action.

24.1 A Candy Man

1. to set down as a rule or a direction to be followed; to order, especially the use of a medicine; to direct _____

2. to surrender; to give in _____

3. to make larger or more powerful; to increase; to enlarge _____

4. to look at thoughtfully; to consider; to ponder _____

5. to give sanction to; to confirm; to approve _____

6. to do a service or favor for; to oblige; to assist _____

7. to form a circle or ring around; to surround; to enclose _____

8. to decide or settle, for example a question or argument; to find out; to resolve _____

9. to gain mastery over; to be greater in strength or influence; to triumph _____

10. to protect from loss; to use carefully; to avoid waste; to save; to preserve _____

Answers

R. capitulate   S. contemplate   N. conserve   C. prescribe   A. ratify

T. amplify   K. prevail   H. accommodate B. determine   E. encompass

$$\underline{\quad}\ \underline{\quad}\ \underline{\quad}\ \underline{\quad}\ \underline{\quad}\ \quad \overset{\text{I}}{\underline{\quad}}\quad \underline{\quad}\ \underline{\quad}\ \underline{\quad}\ \underline{\quad}\ \underline{\quad}\ \underline{\quad}\ \underline{\quad}\ \underline{\quad}$$

3   6   7   4   10   1   9   7   2   4   8   5   2

24.2 A Different Method for Growing Plants

This method is used for growing plants in a solution of water and nutrients without soil. What is it called?

To answer the question, find the phrase that defines each word below. Choose your answers from the phrases after each word. Write the letter of each answer in the space above the word's number at the bottom of the page.

1. capitulate: R. to increase   E. to confirm   N. to surrender

2. encompass: N. to save   S. to surround   D. to assist

3. ratify: E. to resolve   I. to approve   M. to order

4. prevail: P. to make larger   A. to give in   H. to gain mastery over

5. amplify: R. to enlarge   M. to decide   A. to confirm

6. contemplate: P. to consider   S. to assist   W. to direct

7. conserve: E. to approve   O. to save   I. to ponder

8. prescribe: N. to increase   S. to ponder   D. to order

9. determine: C. to decide   O. to approve   E. to order

10. accommodate: Y. to assist   E. to surrender   I. to confirm

— — — — — — — — — — —
4 10 8 5 7 6 7 1 3 9 2

24.3 The Three Musketeers

Alexandre Dumas wrote *The Three Musketeers* in 1844. What were the names of the three musketeers?

To answer the question, read each sentence below. Replace each underlined word or phrase with the word that has a similar meaning. Write the letter of each answer in the space above its sentence number at the bottom of the page. Some letters are provided.

1. Although my brother held me down firmly in our wrestling match, I would not give in.
   H. approve   T. capitulate   R. ratify

2. Ancient astronomers would contemplate the movement of the stars and planets.
   H. ponder   M. conserve   R. capitulate

3. You can use a magnifying glass to amplify an image.
   E. ratify   U. preserve   A. enlarge

4. The champion boxer told his fans that he would prevail over any opponents.
   R. triumph   N. capitulate   I. resolve

5. Doctors consider a patient's symptoms before they order the use of medicine.
   M. accommodate H. prescribe   R. assist

6. A high wall was built to encompass the secret research building.
   E. ponder   A. resolve   I. enclose

7. I save energy by turning off electrical devices when they are not in use.
   E. oblige   O. conserve   I. enlarge

8. Whenever my grandparents come to visit, we assist them in any way we can.
   T. contemplate A. accommodate I. confirm

9. Before a treaty goes into effect, the U.S. Senate must approve it.
   N. triumph   S. encompass   P. ratify

10. We tried to decide whether the old treasure map was real or fake.
    A. determine   T. prescribe   Y. amplify

```
___  ___  T   O   S,   ___  ___  ___  O   S,   ___  R   ___  M   S
 9    7   4       2      10   1   5          8        3        6
```

Action Words, II

English words that express action are a major category of verbs. They add strength and vigor to speaking and writing.

1. collaborate (v): to work together; to cooperate

   All members of the group should be willing to <u>collaborate</u>.

2. recommend (v): to praise or commend someone as being worthy; to endorse; to advise

   Mrs. Johnson is happy with Dana as a babysitter and will <u>recommend</u> her to others.

3. replenish (v): to fill or make complete again; to restore

   The recent heavy rains will <u>replenish</u> the reservoirs.

4. reinforce (v): to strengthen; to increase in number

   After the minor earthquake, we had to <u>reinforce</u> the foundation of our house.

5. bestow (v): to present as a gift or honor; to confer; to grant

   The mayor will <u>bestow</u> medals on the police officers for their heroism.

6. comply (v): to act in accordance with another's command, wish, or rule; to obey

   The boss expected all employees to <u>comply</u> with the company's policies.

7. diminish (v): to make smaller or less; to become smaller or less; to decrease

   By evening the intensity of the snowstorm started to <u>diminish</u>.

8. eradicate (v): to get rid of completely; to eliminate

   It is the hope of modern medicine to <u>eradicate</u> disease.

9. negotiate (v): to bargain with another to reach an agreement; to arrange or settle

   Representatives for both sides will <u>negotiate</u> the new contract.

10. distort (v): to twist or bend out of shape; to give a false or misleading account of; to misrepresent

    The storm was strong enough to <u>distort</u> TV and radio reception.

> ### Vocabulary Tip
>
> **L**inking verbs are a special type of verb. They do not express action but rather link the subject of a sentence with a word in the predicate. Words such as *am, is, was, are,* and *were* are linking verbs.

97

25.1 A Sneeze-Causing Plant

Many people have an allergy to the pollen of ragweed. And a single ragweed plant produces a lot of pollen. About how much pollen can a single ragweed plant produce?

To answer the question, match each definition with its word. Choose your answers from the words after the definitions. Write the letter of each answer in the space above its definition number at the bottom of the page. You will need to divide the letters into words.

1. to act in accordance with another's command, wish, or rule; to obey _____

2. to fill or make complete again; to restore _____

3. to twist or bend out of shape; to give a false or misleading account of; to misrepresent _____

4. to get rid of completely; to eliminate _____

5. to make smaller or less; to become smaller or less; to decrease _____

6. to work together; to cooperate _____

7. to strengthen; to increase in number _____

8. to bargain with another to reach an agreement; to arrange or settle _____

9. to present as a gift or honor; to confer; to grant _____

10. to praise or commend someone as being worthy; to endorse; to advise _____

Answers

E. distort   R. negotiate   A. eradicate   B. reinforce   S. replenish
O. collaborate   N. recommend   G. comply   L. bestow   I. diminish

— — — — — — — — — — — — — — — —
6 10 3 7 5 9 9 5 6 10 1 8 4 5 10 2

25.2 Candy Maker

This chef specializes in making candy. What is this chef called?

To answer the question, find the phrase that defines each word below. Choose your answers from the phrases after each word. Write the letter of each answer in the space above the word's number at the bottom of the page. Some letters are provided.

1. replenish: O. to restore   E. to eliminate   A. to obey

2. distort: N. to rule   S. to overcome   R. to misrepresent

3. eradicate: T. to cooperate   N. to eliminate   L. to restore

4. negotiate: U. to endorse   O. to bargain   H. to twist

5. diminish: E. to decrease   U. to fill   N. to settle

6. collaborate: M. to advise   T. to grant   F. to cooperate

7. comply: C. to obey   S. to grant   W. to restore

8. reinforce: T. to arrange   C. to strengthen   M. to mislead

9. recommend: R. to cooperate   O. to restore   N. to endorse

10. bestow: K. to bargain   T. to confer   V. to obey

___ ___ ___ ___ _E_ ___ ___ _I_ ___ ___ ___ ___
 8   4   9   6   7   10   1   3   5   2

99

25.3 Andromeda

Andromeda is a constellation in the sky above the Northern Hemisphere. Who was Andromeda in Greek mythology?

To answer the question, read each sentence below. Replace each underlined word or phrase with the word that has a similar meaning. Choose your answers from the words after each sentence. Write the letter of each answer in the space above its sentence number at the bottom of the page. You will need to divide the letters into words. Some letters are provided.

1. James tried to give a misleading account of what really happened.
   R. reinforce   N. recommend   A. distort

2. The two authors decided to work together on a new novel.
   H. collaborate   S. negotiate   L. comply

3. Visitors to the wildlife park must act in accordance with the park's safety rules.
   I. eliminate   R. collaborate   T. comply

4. The king will bestow knighthood on the brave warrior.
   D. strengthen   Q. advise   P. confer

5. Patrick tried to arrange his fee for shoveling snow for Mrs. Martin.
   E. negotiate   A. collaborate   U. comply

6. Rest will restore Annie's strength after she runs the marathon.
   N. replenish   H. eliminate   T. negotiate

7. Once the storm passes, the winds will diminish.
   U. confer   O. decrease   E. restore

8. We worked all day to eradicate the weeds from the flower beds.
   H. increase   R. eliminate   A. settle

9. I asked our librarian to advise me of a book I could read for my book report.
   U. collaborate   E. replenish   I. recommend

10. More men were needed to increase the number of the castle's defenders.
    O. distort   S. reinforce   T. bestow

___ ___ ___ ___ C ___ ___ ___ ___ F ___ ___ ___ ___ ___ ___ ___ ___ ___
 4   8   9   6   5   10   10   7   5   3   2   9   7   4   9   1

Action Words, III

English words that express action are a major category of verbs. They add strength and vigor to speaking and writing.

1. refute (v): to prove to be false; to disprove

   The defense attorney tried to <u>refute</u> the charges against her client.

2. verify (v): to prove the truth or accuracy of something; to confirm

   Astronomers sought to <u>verify</u> the recent discovery of an Earthlike planet.

3. unify (v): to combine into a unit; to become or cause to be one; to unite

   Colonial leaders worked to <u>unify</u> the thirteen colonies.

4. suppress (v): to put an end to forcibly; to hold back

   The dictator attempted to <u>suppress</u> his opposition.

5. assert (v): to state or express positively; to affirm; to declare

   We listened to the governor <u>assert</u> that the state was prepared for the coming snowstorm.

6. obliterate (v): to destroy completely; to demolish

   In the movie, a massive asteroid threatened to <u>obliterate</u> New York City.

7. refuse (v): to decline to do something; to reject

   Whenever she is angry, the child will <u>refuse</u> to do whatever she is asked.

8. abstain (v): to refrain from something by choice; to avoid

   Some students will <u>abstain</u> from eating the school lunches because of the new menu.

9. vanquish (v): to defeat or conquer; to overcome

   The powerful invaders will <u>vanquish</u> anyone who dares stand against them.

10. appease (v): to calm, especially by giving something that is wanted; to pacify; to placate

    The mother had to <u>appease</u> the fitful toddler by giving him a new toy.

Vocabulary Tip

Most English verbs form their past tense by adding *-ed*. Irregular verbs have various past forms.

26.1 The First Loser

This man was the first person to lose a U.S. presidential election. (He did later go on to become president.) Who was he?

To answer the question, match each definition with its word. Choose your answers from the words after the definitions. Write the letter of each answer in the space above its definition number at the bottom of the page. You will need to divide the letters into words. Some letters are provided.

1. to decline to do something; to reject _____

2. to defeat or conquer; to overcome _____

3. to prove to be false; to disprove _____

4. to state or express positively; to affirm; to declare _____

5. to refrain from something by choice; to avoid _____

6. to prove the truth or accuracy of a thing; to confirm _____

7. to put an end to forcibly; to hold back _____

8. to calm, especially by giving something that is wanted; to pacify; to placate _____

9. to destroy completely; to demolish _____

10. to combine into a unit; to become or cause to be one; to unite _____

Answers

M. unify   O. assert   J. appease   E. refuse   F. suppress

R. refute   H. verify   S. abstain   T. obliterate   A. vanquish

__	__	__	__	__	__	__	E	__	__	__	__	__	__	N
9	6	4	10	2	5	8		7	7	1	3	5	4	

26.2 An American Cookbook

1. unify: H. to reject   E. to subdue   I. to unite

2. appease: A. to calm   O. to avoid   W. to confirm

3. abstain: O. to avoid   L. to affirm   R. to pacify

4. assert: K. to combine   E. to declare   F. to disprove

5. vanquish: O. to hold back   M. to defeat   L. to confirm

6. refuse: W. to disprove   G. to placate   N. to decline

7. obliterate: E. to prove   A. to hold back   L. to destroy completely

8. refute: K. to decline   I. to confirm   A. to disprove

9. suppress: N. to avoid   S. to hold back   T. to combine

10. verify: M. to confirm   L. to destroy   D. to pacify

___ ___ ___ ___ I ___   ___ ___ ___ M ___ ___ S
 8   10   4   7   2   9   1   5   3   6

26.3 Big News Via Telegraph

This president's inauguration was the first to be reported by telegraph. Who was this president?

To answer the question, complete each sentence with the correct word. Choose your answers from the words after the sentences. Write the letter of each answer in the space above its sentence number at the bottom of the page. You will need to divide the letters into words. One letter is provided.

1. Scientists tried to _____ the exact location of the earthquake.

2. It is usually better to avoid bullies rather than try to _____ them.

3. People feared that the erupting volcano would _____ the town.

4. Colin always finds a way to _____ his opponents in video games.

5. To lose weight, Shane plans to _____ from eating any desserts.

6. I _____ to open any suspicious e-mails.

7. The teacher encouraged the shy student to _____ herself when giving her speech.

8. The company sought to _____ information about problems with its products.

9. During the debate, both teams attempted to _____ their opponent's arguments.

10. The barbarian leader hoped to _____ the different tribes into one.

Answers

| J. refuse | K. refute | O. assert | N. appease | P. suppress |
| E. obliterate | A. verify | X. vanquish | M. unify | L. abstain |

| __ | __ | __ | __ | S | __ | __ | __ | __ | __ | __ | __ | __ |
| 6 | 1 | 10 | 3 | | 9 | 2 | 7 | 4 | 8 | 7 | 5 | 9 |

Action Words, IV

English words that express action are a major category of verbs. They add strength and vigor to speaking and writing.

1. saunter (v): to walk at a leisurely pace; to stroll

    People <u>saunter</u> along the boardwalk on summer evenings.

2. pulverize (v): to reduce to powder or dust by crushing; to demolish

    Mining companies sometimes <u>pulverize</u> rocks to obtain valuable minerals.

3. lubricate (v): to apply a substance to make a thing slippery or smooth; to oil or grease

    Claudia helped her father <u>lubricate</u> the wheels of the lawn mower.

4. infuriate (v): to make very angry; to enrage

    I sometimes think my little brother likes to <u>infuriate</u> me.

5. hover (v): to remain floating or suspended in the air; to remain or linger nearby

    Rhiannon watched a hummingbird <u>hover</u> near a flower.

6. engulf (v): to surround and enclose completely; to overwhelm

    The incoming fog from the sea would soon <u>engulf</u> the town.

7. accelerate (v): to increase the speed of; to move or become faster; to quicken

    We watched the race cars <u>accelerate</u> toward the finish line.

8. persevere (v): to persist in any purpose; to strive in spite of difficulties; to endure

    Alison will <u>persevere</u> in her dream to be a writer someday.

9. culminate (v): to reach the highest point or degree; to conclude

    Our final year in middle school will <u>culminate</u> in graduation.

10. designate (v): to indicate or specify; to point out; to appoint

    Blue dots on the road map <u>designate</u> rest areas.

Vocabulary Tip

Choose strong action words to express your ideas.

27.1 Chimpanzees

This woman is known for her tireless study of chimpanzees. Who is she?

To answer the question, match each definition with its word. Choose your answer from the words after each definition. Write the letter of each answer in the space above its definition number at the bottom of the page. One letter is provided.

1. to increase the speed of; to move or become faster; to quicken _____
   E. saunter   A. accelerate   Y. lubricate

2. to indicate or specify; to point out; to appoint _____
   O. infuriate   E. culminate   A. designate

3. to remain floating or suspended in the air; to remain or linger nearby _____
   M. accelerate   D. hover   S. persevere

4. to walk at a leisurely pace; to stroll _____
   N. saunter   R. accelerate   I. culminate

5. to make very angry; to enrage _____
   A. designate   I. pulverize   O. infuriate

6. to reach the highest point or degree; to conclude _____
   S. engulf   L. hover   J. culminate

7. to reduce to powder or dust by crushing; to demolish _____
   L. pulverize   S. designate   E. infuriate

8. to surround and enclose completely; to overwhelm _____
   S. culminate   E. engulf   A. hover

9. to apply a substance to make slippery or smooth; to oil or grease _____
   G. lubricate   M. accelerate   R. saunter

10. to persist in any purpose; to strive in spite of difficulties; to endure _____
    Y. hover   E. infuriate   L. persevere

___ ___ ___ ___   ___ ___   O   ___ ___ ___ ___
6   1   4   8   9   5   ___   3   2   10 7

27.2 Ohio

The name *Ohio* comes from an Iroquoian word. What did *Ohio* originally mean?

To answer the question, find the phrase that best defines each word below. Choose your answers from the phrases after each word. Write the letter of each answer in the space above the word's number at the bottom of the page. You will need to divide the letters into words.

1. pulverize: I. to demolish   E. to appoint   A. to quicken

2. engulf: A. to point out   E. to overwhelm   O. to remain nearby

3. accelerate: T. to quicken   M. to enrage   I. to conclude

4. persevere: I. to make slippery   E. to endure   O. to enrage

5. designate: R. to appoint   U. to stroll   S. to strive

6. culminate: S. to overwhelm   N. to enrage   R. to conclude

7. lubricate: L. to increase   G. to make slippery   C. to surround

8. hover: H. to conclude   R. to float in the air   I. to reduce

9. infuriate: T. to strive   N. to point out   V. to enrage

10. saunter: I. to conclude   U. to quicken   A. to walk leisurely

___ ___ ___ ___ ___ ___ ___ ___ ___ ___
 7   8   2   10   3   5   1   9   4   6

27.3 A First for the U.S. Congress

This woman was the first African American woman elected to the U.S. Congress. Who was she?

To answer the question, complete each sentence with the correct word. Choose your answers from the words after the sentences. Write the letter of each answer in the space above its sentence number at the bottom of the page.

1. A rocket must _____ to a high speed to escape the Earth's gravity.

2. The owner of the company will _____ his daughter as his successor.

3. Ernesto will _____ the hinges on the fence's gate so that it opens smoothly.

4. Teasing an animal can _____ him.

5. My presentation about the Mayans will _____ in a slide show.

6. Deer frequently _____ through our backyard.

7. The firefighters arrived just as the flames were about to _____ the house.

8. Math is a hard subject for Shane, but he promised himself that he would _____ and earn a passing grade.

9. The big wrecking ball will quickly _____ the old building.

10. Unlike a plane, a helicopter can _____ over a spot.

Answers

C. engulf   H. pulverize   S. accelerate   L. persevere   I. saunter
O. designate   M. lubricate   E. hover   R. culminate   Y. infuriate

__ __ __ __ __ __ __   __ __ __ __ __ __ __ __
 1 9 6 5 8 10 4   7 9 6 1 9 2 8 3

Descriptive Words, I

Descriptive words can add details to sentences. They add interest to expression.

1. conventional (adj): arising from general usage or custom; customary

    We celebrate the Fourth of July in a <u>conventional</u> manner, first with a picnic and then attending a fireworks show.

2. eerie (adj): inspiring fear or dread; weird

    Alana trembled at the <u>eerie</u> light coming from the old, abandoned house.

3. arrogant (adj): overly convinced of one's own importance; overbearing; haughty; conceited

    John is <u>arrogant</u> and believes he is better than other students.

4. exclusive (adj): intended for or possessed by a single person or group; private

    We had <u>exclusive</u> backstage tickets that allowed us to meet the concert's stars.

5. judicious (adj): having or exercising good judgment; prudent

    Liza is a <u>judicious</u> student who will make an excellent student council president.

6. potential (adj): possible; latent

    <u>Potential</u> snowfall amounts from the storm could exceed two feet.

7. strenuous (adj): requiring or characterized by great effort or exertion; arduous

    Russell was exhausted after a two-hour, <u>strenuous</u> workout in the gym.

8. belligerent (adj): eager to fight; hostile; aggressive; quarrelsome

    When Robert is in a bad mood, he becomes <u>belligerent</u>.

9. indisputable (adj): undeniable; irrefutable; incontestable; evident

    With the empty cookie wrapper by his pillow, it was <u>indisputable</u> that my dog had eaten my snack.

10. exorbitant (adj): exceeding the usual and proper limits; excessive; extravagant

    The price of the tickets to the championship game was <u>exorbitant</u>.

> **Vocabulary Tip**
>
> **A**djectives and adverbs are descriptive words.

109

28.1 In Pursuit of Atoms

This scientist is often referred to as the father of nuclear physics for his study of atoms. Who was he?

To answer the question, match each definition with its word. Choose your answers from the words after the definitions. Write the letter of each answer in the space above its definition number at the bottom of the page.

1. having or exercising good judgment; prudent _____

2. requiring or characterized by great effort or exertion; arduous _____

3. exceeding the usual and proper limits; excessive; extravagant _____

4. eager to fight; hostile; aggressive _____

5. overly convinced of one's own importance; overbearing; haughty; conceited _____

6. arising from general usage or custom; customary _____

7. possible; latent _____

8. undeniable; irrefutable; incontestable; evident _____

9. intended for or possessed by a single person or group; private _____

10. inspiring fear or dread; weird _____

Answers

S. judicious   D. conventional   R. eerie   T. potential   H. strenuous
O. indisputable   U. belligerent   N. arrogant   E. exclusive   F. exorbitant

— — — — — —   — — — — — — — — — —
9 10 5 9 1 7   10 4 7 2 9 10 3 8 10 6

28.2 Grenada

Grenada is an island located in the Caribbean Sea. It is a leading producer of a certain product and is sometimes referred to by a special name. What is Grenada's special name?

To answer the question, complete each sentence with the correct word. Choose your answers from the words after the sentences. Write the letter of each answer in the space above its sentence number at the bottom of the page. You will need to divide the letters into words. One letter is provided.

1. Carrying the heavy new sofa into the house was a _____ job.

2. We found the high fees for parking in the city to be _____.

3. Our family is quite ordinary and shares _____ attitudes on most issues.

4. Based on the instant replay, it was _____ that the runner stepped out of bounds.

5. The _____ nobleman felt that he was born to rule.

6. The _____ movie gave Erica nightmares.

7. The _____ tribe was always at war with its neighbors.

8. The _____ restaurant required reservations to be made weeks in advance.

9. Brad would like to expand his business and is considering new _____ markets.

10. Given the severity of the snowstorm, the decision to close school was _____.

Answers

S. indisputable   I. potential   T. belligerent   N. judicious   H. arrogant
D. exclusive   A. exorbitant   L. eerie   P. strenuous   E. conventional

___ ___ ___ ___ ___ ___   C   ___ ___ ___ ___ ___ ___ ___
7   5   3   4   1   9   3   9   4   6   2   10   8

28.3 Cleaning the Coasts

Since 1986, for one day each year in September, volunteers around the world collect trash and debris at coasts along beaches, lakes, rivers, and other waterways. What is this event called?

To answer the question, read each sentence below. Replace each underlined word with the word that has a similar meaning. Choose your answers from the words after the sentences. Write the letter of each answer in the space above its sentence number at the bottom of the page. Some letters are provided.

1. The prices of clothes in the store were <u>exorbitant</u>.

2. Bailing hay on my grandfather's farm is <u>strenuous</u> work.

3. Tiara's sister had a <u>customary</u> wedding.

4. The <u>private</u> showing of the painter's work was by invitation only.

5. It is an <u>indisputable</u> fact that 2 + 2 = 4.

6. With reports of many accidents, our decision not to drive on the icy roads was <u>prudent</u>.

7. The <u>eerie</u> sound coming from the attic woke Jessica and made her shudder.

8. The <u>potential</u> savings on our monthly electric bill will be about 10 percent if we switch to energy-efficient lightbulbs.

9. Billy has a <u>quarrelsome</u> nature and is always ready for a fight.

10. <u>Haughty</u> people often have few true friends.

Answers

N. arrogant   I. excessive   C. judicious   P. conventional   O. arduous
R. weird   A. belligerent L. possible   T. exclusive   E. undeniable

—	—	—	—	—	—	—	—	—	—	—	—	—
1	10	4	5	7	10	9	4	1	2	10	9	8

—	—	—	S	—	—	—	—	—	—	—	U	—
6	2	9		4	9	8	6	8	5	9	10	3

Descriptive Words, II

Descriptive words can add details to sentences. They add interest to expression.

1. trivial (adj): of little importance; insignificant; trifling

   Elena and her sister sometimes argue over <u>trivial</u> problems.

2. sluggish (adj): displaying little movement; lacking in alertness or energy; slow

   Sara felt <u>sluggish</u> because of her cold.

3. ravenous (adj): extremely hungry; voracious; greedy; predatory

   Having not eaten since breakfast, by evening I was <u>ravenous</u>.

4. prudent (adj): exercising good judgment or common sense; judicious; sensible

   Buying a fuel-efficient car is a <u>prudent</u> decision.

5. intensive (adj): pertaining to great concentration, power, or force; thorough

   Becoming a doctor requires <u>intensive</u> study.

6. controversial (adj): pertaining to a dispute; disputable; arguable

   The <u>controversial</u> decision to eliminate the school's art program upset many students and parents.

7. tedious (adj): tiresome; uninteresting; wearisome; boring

   Matthew always found cleaning his room to be a <u>tedious</u> job.

8. invaluable (adj): priceless; indispensable

   The ring, which had been passed down from Lucy's great grandmother, was <u>invaluable</u>.

9. vital (adj): necessary for life; life-sustaining; essential

   Oxygen, food, water, and shelter are <u>vital</u> to animal life on Earth.

10. predominant (adj): having greater importance, power, or number; superior; paramount

    The Cougars are the <u>predominant</u> team in our conference.

> **Vocabulary Tip**
>
> **W**hen speaking and writing, choose descriptive words that form clear images in the minds of listeners and readers.

29.1 Your Lungs

If you are like most people, your left lung is slightly smaller than your right lung. Why?

To answer the question, match each definition with its word. Choose your answers from the words after the definitions. Write the letter of each answer in the space above its definition number at the bottom of the page. You will need to divide the letters into words. One letter is provided.

1. pertaining to great concentration, power, or force; thorough _____

2. pertaining to a dispute; disputable; arguable _____

3. having greater importance, power, or number; superior; paramount _____

4. exercising good judgment or common sense; judicious; cautious _____

5. necessary for life; life-sustaining; essential _____

6. priceless; indispensable _____

7. extremely hungry; voracious; greedy; predatory _____

8. displaying little movement; lacking in alertness or energy; slow _____

9. of little importance; insignificant; trifling _____

10. tiresome; uninteresting; wearisome; boring _____

Answers

Y. sluggish   H. trivial   O. tedious   E. prudent   M. controversial
U. predominant   T. ravenous   K. intensive   R. vital   A. invaluable

—	—	—	—	—	—	—	—	—	—	F	—	—
7	10	2	6	1	4	5	10	10	2		10	5

—	—	—	—	—	—	—	—
8	10	3	5	9	4	6	5	7

29.2 A Cave Researcher

This person studies caves. What is he or she called?

To answer the question, find the word or phrase that defines each word below. Choose your answers from the words or phrases that follow each word. Write the letter of each answer in the space above the word's number at the bottom of the page. Some letters are provided.

1. tedious
   A. of sound mind
   O. indispensable
   E. tiresome

2. vital
   O. life-sustaining
   I. exercising common sense
   A. paramount

3. ravenous
   S. disputable
   R. uninteresting
   T. extremely hungry

4. intensive
   N. spiteful
   L. thorough
   C. superior

5. sluggish
   O. having greater number
   I. lacking in energy
   U. wearisome

6. predominant
   W. essential
   L. superior
   H. insightful

7. invaluable
   E. thorough
   S. priceless
   O. sensible

8. controversial
   S. pertaining to a dispute
   C. lacking in alertness
   M. insignificant

9. prudent
   J. having greater power
   T. inactive
   G. exercising common sense

10. trivial
    E. thorough
    U. essential
    O. trifling

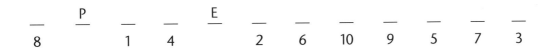

__	P	__	__	E	__	__	__	__	__	__	__
8		1	4		2	6	10	9	5	7	3

29.3 Teeth

Your primary teeth are replaced with permanent teeth. What is another name for your permanent teeth?

To answer the question, complete each sentence with the correct word. Choose your answers from the words after each sentence. Write the letter of each answer in the space above its sentence number at the bottom of the page. Some letters are provided.

1. Our flight was canceled and we spent a _____ night at the airport.
   M. prudent   D. tedious   R. trivial

2. Many biologists agree that lions are the _____ predator.
   N. tedious   S. predominant   D. sluggish

3. The wolf stalked his prey with _____ eyes.
   A. ravenous   U. controversial   O. trivial

4. Saving money for an emergency is _____.
   O. trivial   A. intensive   E. prudent

5. The candidates debated several _____ issues last night.
   Y. sluggish   E. controversial   U. ravenous

6. Having owned a successful business, her grandfather gave Lori _____ advice for starting her own company.
   C. invaluable   R. trifling   M. sluggish

7. In her report, Marlena tried to avoid _____ facts.
   N. prudent   L. ravenous   S. trivial

8. The medical tests provided _____ information about the patient's condition.
   N. controversial   U. vital   S. tedious

9. After having stayed up late, Peter was _____ the next day.
   U. sluggish   A. invaluable   E. prudent

10. The police caught the fugitive after the _____ manhunt.
    U. ravenous   E. invaluable   O. intensive

__ __ __ C __ __ __ N __ __ __ __ teeth
7 9 6   4 1 3   5 10 8 2

Descriptive Words, II

Descriptive Words, III

Descriptive words can add details to sentences. They add interest to expression.

1. inconvenient (adj): not accessible or handy; untimely; troublesome

   The snowstorm's arrival during rush hour was <u>inconvenient</u> for commuters.

2. capacious (adj): capable of containing a large quantity; spacious; roomy

   The new school had a <u>capacious</u> cafeteria.

3. ultimate (adj): final; last; eventual; supreme; greatest

   The <u>ultimate</u> objective in chess is to capture your opponent's king.

4. amiable (adj): having a pleasant disposition; friendly; good-natured

   Jennifer is an <u>amiable</u> girl who always has a smile.

5. renowned (adj): famous; well-known; celebrated; eminent

   Karl is reading the latest book of the <u>renowned</u> author.

6. despondent (adj): feeling or expressing dejection; disheartened; dispirited; depressed

   Kalyn was <u>despondent</u> after breaking her ankle.

7. calamitous (adj): causing or involving a disaster; disastrous; catastrophic

   The eruption of the volcano was <u>calamitous</u> for the island.

8. fallible (adj): capable of making a mistake; liable to be incorrect; imperfect

   Human beings are <u>fallible</u> creatures.

9. mutual (adj): having the same relationship or attitude toward each other; reciprocal

   The two rival teams share mutual <u>respect</u>.

10. available (adj): capable of being used; at hand; accessible; handy

    When the power went out, we used every <u>available</u> flashlight in our house.

> **Vocabulary Tip**
>
> **A**nother name for descriptive words is modifiers.

30.1 The Hairs on Your Head

The average person has a lot of hairs on his or her head. About how many hairs are on the average human scalp?

To answer the question, match each definition with its word. Choose your answers from the words after the definitions. Write the letter of each answer in the space above its definition number at the bottom of the page. You will need to divide the letters into words.

1. causing or involving a disaster; disastrous; catastrophic _____

2. final; last; eventual; supreme; greatest _____

3. famous; well-known; celebrated; eminent _____

4. capable of being used; at hand; accessible; handy _____

5. capable of making a mistake; liable to be incorrect; imperfect _____

6. not accessible or handy; untimely; troublesome _____

7. feeling or expressing dejection; disheartened; dispirited; depressed _____

8. having the same relationship or attitude to each other; reciprocal _____

9. capable of containing a large quantity; spacious; roomy _____

10. having a pleasant disposition; friendly; good-natured _____

Answers

H. available	N. amiable	R. calamitous	D. despondent	U. ultimate
O. mutual	S. fallible	E. capacious	A. renowned	T. inconvenient

— — —   — — — — — — —   — — — — — — — —
8 10 9   4 2 10 7 1 9 7   6 4 8 2 5 3 10 7

30.2 A Book Collector

People who collect books are known by a special name. What is this name?
  To answer the question, complete each sentence with the correct word. Choose your answers from the words after each sentence. Write the letter of each answer in the space above its sentence number at the bottom of the page. One letter is provided.

1. My father was glad that replacement parts for our old snow blower were _____.
   L. calamitous   R. capacious   P. available

2. The students at Carlo's new school are _____ and he has made many friends.
   B. amiable   N. despondent   U. inconvenient

3. The _____ storm left thousands of people without electricity for days.
   U. mutual   I. calamitous   A. fallible

4. For most people, being without a cell phone for a whole day is very _____.
   I. inconvenient   U. available   O. fallible

5. Thomas Edison was a _____ inventor.
   N. capacious   S. mutual   E. renowned

6. In Rashid's opinion, the New York Yankees are the _____ baseball team.
   R. amiable   B. ultimate   M. capacious

7. Rebecca and Charlene were introduced by a _____ friend.
   S. calamitous   H. mutual   U. capacious

8. Ervin's father told him that everyone is _____ and makes mistakes.
   L. fallible   R. capacious   W. mutual

9. More than a thousand people attended the concert in the _____ theater.
   U. inconvenient   I. capacious   E. mutual

10. The team was _____ after losing the championship game.
    E. calamitous   O. fallible   L. despondent

___ ___ ___ ___ ___   O   ___ ___ ___ ___ ___
 6   9   2   8   4   ‾‾   1   7   3   10   5

30.3 An Ancient City

Many historians believe that this city, which was flourishing at least 3,500 years ago, is one of the oldest (if not the oldest!) continuously inhabited city in the world. What city is this and in what country is it located?

To answer the question, read each sentence below. Replace the underlined word with a word that has a similar meaning. Choose your answers from the words after each sentence. Write the letter of each answer in the space above its sentence number at the bottom of the page. Some letters are provided.

1. The greatest vacation for Jared would be a trip around the world.
   S. ultimate   U. available   L. capacious

2. Everyone feels depressed occasionally.
   N. inconvenient   A. despondent   T. mutual

3. The closing of the factory was a calamitous event for the town.
   U. reciprocal   I. handy   A. disastrous

4. We went to an exhibit of a renowned artist's paintings.
   U. famous   O. capacious   A. good-natured

5. The two scientists share a reciprocal admiration for each other's work.
   R. dispirited   P. calamitous   M. mutual

6. Students feel that Mrs. Morgan is the most amiable teacher in the school.
   E. untimely   Y. good-natured   A. fallible

7. Because of our early flight, we had to leave our home at an untimely hour.
   K. available   M. amiable   C. inconvenient

8. Our room at the hotel was capacious.
   D. spacious   B. amiable   C. catastrophic

9. A wise person understands that he or she is fallible.
   O. despondent   I. imperfect   R. celebrated

10. The ingredients Tina needed to bake the cake were available in the cupboards.
    S. handy   C. disheartened   I. roomy

___ ___ ___ A ___ ___ ___ S,   ___ ___ R ___ ___
 8   3   5   1   7   4   10 6   9   2

Descriptive Words, III

120

Descriptive Words, IV

Descriptive words can add details to sentences. They add interest to expression.

1. ample (adj): of large or great size; in abundant measure; substantial; extensive

   Our new house had <u>ample</u> space for four people.

2. random (adj): having no specific pattern; haphazard

   A <u>random</u> poll found that 60 percent of the students in our school preferred pizza for lunch.

3. notorious (adj): Widely known and usually disapproved of; infamous

   Jesse James was a <u>notorious</u> outlaw of the Old West.

4. fluent (adj): capable of speaking and writing effortlessly; flowing smoothly; graceful

   Lora's aunt is <u>fluent</u> in three languages.

5. plausible (adj): seeming to be valid or acceptable; believable; likely

   Scientists sought a <u>plausible</u> explanation for the strange lights in the sky.

6. celestial (adj): of or pertaining to the sky or heaven; heavenly; divine

   In many cultures, angels are believed to be <u>celestial</u> beings.

7. genial (adj): having a friendly disposition or manner; kindly

   Rosa is a <u>genial</u> person and has a lot of friends.

8. cynical (adj): distrusting of the virtues of others; sneering; sarcastic

   James is <u>cynical</u> and refuses to see the good in people.

9. boisterous (adj): noisy and unrestrained; uproarious; stormy

   Kim was exhausted after babysitting the <u>boisterous</u> twins.

10. dexterous (adj): skillful use of the hands, body, or mind; deft; adroit

    The pianist's <u>dexterous</u> fingers seemed to dance across the keyboard.

Vocabulary Tip

The right descriptive words can help you to express your ideas clearly.

31.1 Your Blood Vessels

Your blood vessels carry oxygen and food to every cell in your body. They also carry wastes away from your cells to be excreted. About how many miles of blood vessels does the average human adult have?

To answer the question, match each definition with its word. Choose your answers from the words after the definitions. Write the letter of each answer in the space above its definition number at the bottom of the page. You will need to divide the letters into words. One letter is provided.

1. distrusting of the virtues of others; sneering; sarcastic _____

2. skillful use of the hands, body, or mind; deft; adroit _____

3. capable of speaking and writing effortlessly; flowing smoothly; graceful _____

4. having a friendly disposition or manner; kindly _____

5. of large or great size; in abundant measure; substantial; extensive _____

6. seeming to be valid or acceptable; believable; likely _____

7. noisy and unrestrained; uproarious; stormy _____

8. of or pertaining to the sky or heaven; heavenly; divine _____

9. having no specific pattern; haphazard _____

10. widely known and usually disapproved of; infamous _____

Answers

I. boisterous	X. notorious	U. fluent	N. random	Y. cynical
H. dexterous	T. ample	O. celestial	S. genial	A. plausible

___ ___ ___ ___ ___ ___ ___ ___ ___ ___ ___ ___ $\frac{D}{}$
4   7   10   5   1   5   2   8   3   4   6   9

31.2 A Secret

A thing written in code has a special name. What is this name?

   To answer the question, read each sentence below. Replace each under-lined word or phrase with the word or phrase that has a similar meaning. Choose your answers from the words or phrases after each sentence. Write the letter of each answer in the space above its sentence number at the bottom of the page.

1. The fans cheered for their team during the uproarious pep rally.
   E. adroit   T. boisterous   M. cynical

2. Mr. Lee is genial and always greets everyone with a smile.
   U. dexterous   O. cynical   A. kindly

3. We packed substantial supplies for our camping trip.
   O. uproarious   T. notorious   R. ample

4. Lex Luthor, Superman's archenemy, is an infamous villain.
   P. notorious   J. cynical   S. unrestrained

5. The audience applauded the ballerina's fluent movements.
   U. celestial   R. graceful   M. plausible

6. The storm uprooted trees in a haphazard manner.
   E. a cynical   A. an extensive   O. a random

7. Stars and planets are sometimes referred to as heavenly bodies.
   E. boisterous   Y. celestial   O. substantial

8. Sarcastic people sometimes say things that others find hurtful.
   C. Cynical   T. Infamous   K. Dexterous

9. Tommy did not have a believable excuse for not finishing his work.
   M. plausible   R. notorious   D. haphazard

10. The deft clown easily turned the balloon into a rabbit.
    W. genial   G. dexterous   R. divine

| __ | __ | __ | __ | __ | __ | __ | __ | __ | __ |
| 8 | 3 | 7 | 4 | 1 | 6 | 10 | 5 | 2 | 9 |

31.3 A Special Science

This science deals with the motion of projectiles. What is the name of this science?

To answer the question, read each sentence below. If the underlined word is used correctly, write the letter for correct in the space above its sentence number at the bottom of the page. If the underlined word is not used correctly, write the letter for incorrect.

1. Astronomers study <u>celestial</u> objects.
   I. correct   E. incorrect

2. A <u>cynical</u> person usually appreciates the goodness in others.
   U. correct   I. incorrect

3. The <u>genial</u> tour guide made our trip enjoyable.
   T. correct   N. incorrect

4. The police could not catch the <u>notorious</u> jewel thief.
   L. correct   O. incorrect

5. The reason for my high cell phone bill was <u>plausible</u> and made no sense.
   N. correct   S. incorrect

6. The <u>boisterous</u> audience listened quietly and politely to the debate.
   U. correct   A. incorrect

7. Alicia is <u>fluent</u> in English and Spanish.
   C. correct   K. incorrect

8. Marissa has an <u>ample</u> supply of pens, pencils, and papers for schoolwork.
   B. correct   T. incorrect

9. The tree's <u>dexterous</u> branches moved gracefully in the wind.
   M. correct   S. incorrect

10. Jason plays a specific sequence of <u>random</u> numbers in his state's lottery.
    O. correct   L. incorrect

___   ___   ___   ___   ___   ___   ___   ___   ___   ___
 8   6   10   4   1   9   3   2   7   5

Compound Words, I

A compound word is formed from two or more words. Compound words may be closed (for example, outcome), open (rush hour), or hyphenated (far-fetched).

1. whirlwind (n): a column of violently rotating air; a tornado

   The <u>whirlwind</u> scattered branches and leaves across the yard.

2. waterfront (n): land bordering a natural body of water

   The seafood restaurant was located on the city's <u>waterfront</u>.

3. outcome (n): a result; a consequence; an effect

   The <u>outcome</u> of our science experiment showed that matter expands when heated.

4. far-fetched (adj): improbable; unlikely; implausible

   Mika offered a <u>far-fetched</u> excuse for not completing her report.

5. lightheaded (adj): delirious; giddy; faint

   Being outside in the heat and humidity all day made Katelyn feel <u>lightheaded</u>.

6. downpour (n): a heavy fall of rain

   We got caught in a <u>downpour</u> while walking to school and arrived sopping wet.

7. makeshift (adj): pertaining to something used as a temporary or improvised substitute

   My grandfather told me how to use a stick, string, and hook as a <u>makeshift</u> fishing pole.

8. rush hour (n): a period of high traffic

   rush-hour (adj): pertaining to a period of heavy traffic

   To get to the game on time, we had to drive to the city during <u>rush hour</u>.

   Dad tries to avoid <u>rush-hour</u> traffic when driving to work.

9. drawbridge (n): a structure that can be raised or drawn aside to permit or prevent passage

   The only way over the moat and into the castle was across the <u>drawbridge</u>.

10. frostbite (n): tissue damage as a result of freezing

    To avoid <u>frostbite</u>, you should wear warm clothing.

> ### Vocabulary Tip
>
> **U**nderstanding the meanings of the words that form a compound word can provide clues to the compound word's meaning.

32.1 Cartoon Sorcerer

In Disney's cartoon feature *Fantasia*, the sorcerer's name is Yensid. Where did the name Yensid come from?

To answer the question, match each definition with its word. Choose your answers from the words after the definitions. Write the letter of each answer in the space above its definition number at the bottom of the page. You will need to divide the letters into words. Some letters are provided.

1. a period of high traffic _____

2. improbable; unlikely; implausible _____

3. a heavy fall of rain _____

4. tissue damage as a result of freezing _____

5. a column of violently rotating air; a tornado _____

6. a structure that can be raised or drawn aside to permit or prevent passage _____

7. delirious; giddy; faint _____

8. pertaining to something used as a temporary or improvised substitute _____

9. land bordering a natural body of water _____

10. a result; a consequence; an effect _____

Answers

I. lightheaded	D. waterfront	L. whirlwind	B. rush hour	A. downpour
Y. far-fetched	E. makeshift	S. outcome	W. frostbite	K. drawbridge

$$\underset{9}{\_\_} \ \underset{7}{\_\_} \ \underset{10}{\_\_} \ \underset{}{\overset{N}{\_\_}} \quad \underset{8}{\_\_} \ \underset{2}{\_\_} \ \underset{10}{\_\_} \ \underset{}{\overset{P}{\_\_}} \quad \underset{8}{\_\_} \ \underset{5}{\_\_} \ \underset{5}{\_\_} \ \underset{8}{\_\_} \ \underset{9}{\_\_}$$

$$\underset{1}{\_\_} \ \underset{3}{\_\_} \ \underset{6}{\overset{C}{\_\_}} \quad \underset{4}{\_\_} \ \underset{3}{\_\_} \ \underset{9}{\overset{R}{\_\_}}$$

32.2 First Televised Presidential Debate

The first televised debate between candidates for U.S. president was broadcast in 1960. Who were the candidates?

To answer the question, match each word on the left with the key words of its definition on the right. Write the letter of each answer in the space above the word's number at the bottom of the page. You will need to divide the letters into words. Some letters are provided.

Words

1. downpour _____

2. drawbridge _____

3. makeshift _____

4. outcome _____

5. far-fetched _____

6. rush hour _____

7. whirlwind _____

8. lightheaded _____

9. waterfront _____

10. frostbite _____

Key Words of Definitions

E. a temporary or improvised substitute

H. improbable or unlikely

N. tissue damage because of freezing

J. column of violently rotating air

D. land bordering water

R. a result

I. delirious; giddy; faint

Y. heavy rain

X. time of heavy traffic

O. structure that permits or prevents passage by being raised or drawn aside

$$\underline{}_{7} \quad \underline{}_{2} \quad \underline{}_{5} \quad \underline{}_{10} \quad \underline{K}_{} \quad \underline{}_{3} \quad \underline{}_{10} \quad \underline{}_{10} \quad \underline{}_{3} \quad \underline{}_{9} \quad \underline{}_{1}'$$

$$\underline{}_{4} \quad \underline{}_{8} \quad \underline{C}_{5} \quad \underline{}_{} \quad \underline{A}_{} \quad \underline{}_{4} \quad \underline{}_{9} \quad \underline{}_{10} \quad \underline{}_{8} \quad \underline{}_{6} \quad \underline{}_{2} \quad \underline{}_{10}$$

32.3 The Stars in the Sky

On a clear night in the Northern Hemisphere, away from the lights of a city or town, a person with good vision can see a lot of stars. About how many stars can a person with good vision see on a clear night, without the use of any telescopic devices?

To answer the question, complete each sentence with the correct word. Choose your answers from the words after the sentences. Write the letter of each answer in the space above its sentence number at the bottom of the page. You will need to divide the letters into words. Some letters are provided.

Compound Words, I

1. The king ordered the _____ raised in defense of the castle.

2. Mom was late for dinner because of the _____ traffic.

3. Sometimes when I stand up too quickly, I become _____.

4. _____ is a danger when you are outside in very cold temperatures.

5. The hotel was on the _____, overlooking the bay.

6. The _____ caused minor street flooding.

7. Tom did not like the story because of its _____ plot.

8. The _____ of the election for student council president was a surprise.

9. A rolled-up newspaper can serve as a _____ fly swatter.

10. We saw leaves and dust blowing around the center of the _____.

Answers

A. waterfront   V. rush-hour   C. lightheaded   F. outcome   U. downpour
S. makeshift   T. far-fetched   E. drawbridge   N. whirlwind   O. frostbite

__ L __ __ __ __ __ __   I __ __ __   H __ __ __ __ __ D
3   4   9   1   7   4   8   2   1   7   4   6   9   5   10

128

Compound Words, II

A compound word is formed from two or more words. Compound words may be closed (for example, landlord), open (alma mater), or hyphenated (bad-tempered).

1. **turtleneck** (n): a high collar that fits around the neck; a garment that has a high collar that fits around the neck; (adj): having a high collar

   Danny's <u>turtleneck</u> keeps him warm on cold days.

   Sherri wore her green <u>turtleneck</u> sweater to the party.

2. **well-to-do** (adj): prosperous; affluent

   The Johnsons are a <u>well-to-do</u> family that owns several businesses in town.

3. **custom-made** (adj): built, created, or produced according to an individual's specifications

   My grandfather has <u>custom-made</u> furniture in his mountain cabin.

4. **alma mater** (n): the school, college, or university one has attended; a school song

   My mother's <u>alma mater</u> is the University of Texas.

5. **old-fashioned** (adj): favoring outdated clothing, ideas, or methods; dated; obsolete

   Some teenagers feel that their parents are <u>old-fashioned</u>.

6. **bad-tempered** (adj): irritable; irascible; quarrelsome

   The old cat was <u>bad-tempered</u> and preferred to be left alone.

7. **landlord** (n): a person who owns and rents out lands, buildings, or apartments; an innkeeper

   Our <u>landlord</u> allows his tenants to keep pets.

8. **showdown** (n): an action that forces an issue to a conclusion

   The game was a <u>showdown</u> between the best two teams in the conference.

9. **brokenhearted** (adj): grievously sad; grief-stricken

   The princess was <u>brokenhearted</u> when she thought the prince was lost to her forever.

10. **seaport** (n): a harbor, town, or city that has facilities for ocean-going ships

    New York City is a major <u>seaport</u>.

Vocabulary Tip

Because language evolves over time, new compound words come into use, and some open and hyphenated compounds can become closed compounds.

33.1 The Chipmunks

Of the four main characters of *The Chipmunks*, Alvin is the star. Who are the other three main characters?

To answer the question, match each definition with its word. Choose your answers from the words after the definitions. Write the letter of each answer in the space above its definition number at the bottom of the page. You will need to divide the letters into words. Some letters are provided.

1. an action that forces an issue to a conclusion _____

2. the school, college, or university one has attended _____

3. a high collar that fits around the neck _____

4. a harbor, town, or city that has facilities for ocean-going ships _____

5. grievously sad; grief-stricken _____

6. favoring outdated clothing, ideas, or methods; dated; obsolete _____

7. built, created, or produced according to an individual's specifications _____

8. irritable; irascible; quarrelsome _____

9. a person who rents out lands, buildings, or apartments; an innkeeper _____

10. prosperous; affluent _____

Answers

D. bad-tempered   A. showdown   T. brokenhearted   N. alma mater   I. seaport
V. old-fashioned   E. turtleneck   M. custom-made   O. well-to-do   S. landlord

__	__	__	__	__	__	H	__	__	__	__	R	__	__	__	__	__
9	4	7	10	2	5		3	10	8	10		3	8	1	6	3

33.2 The First Moon Landing

On July 20, 1969, American astronauts Neil Armstrong and Edwin (Buzz) Aldrin became the first humans to land on the moon. In what region of the moon did they land?

To answer the question, match each word on the left with the key words of its definition on the right. Write the letter of each answer in the space above the word's number at the bottom of the page. You will need to divide the letters into words. Some letters are provided.

Words	**Key Words of Definitions**
1. brokenhearted _____	O. a person who rents out an apartment
2. bad-tempered _____	Q. favoring outdated clothing and ideas
3. custom-made _____	S. prosperous; affluent
4. landlord _____	E. a garment with a high collar
5. alma mater _____	T. a harbor with facilities for ships
6. old-fashioned _____	N. grief-stricken
7. turtleneck _____	I. an action forcing an issue to a conclusion
8. showdown _____	F. irritable; irascible; quarrelsome
9. well-to-do _____	A. the school or college one has attended
10. seaport _____	Y. built according to an individual's specifications

__ __ __ __ __ __ R __ __ __ U __ L __ __ __
9 7 5 4 2 10   5 1 6   8   8 10 3

Compound Words, II

33.3 The Wizard of Oz

In *The Wizard of Oz*, Dorothy meets the Scarecrow, the Cowardly Lion, and the Tin Man. All three are searching for something. What, respectively, is each looking for?

To answer the question, complete each sentence with the correct word. Choose your answers from the words after each sentence. Write the letter of each answer in the space above its sentence number at the bottom of the page. You will need to divide the letters into words. Some letters are provided.

1. The dusty trunk we found in the attic contained _____ clothes.
   U. old-fashioned   A. brokenhearted   E. bad-tempered

2. Bolivia is a landlocked country without a single _____.
   M. showdown   R. landlord   H. seaport

3. Marta was _____ and cried every night until her lost dog was found.
   T. old-fashioned   I. brokenhearted   N. well-to-do

4. To block the cold wind from his throat, Randy wears a _____.
   S. custom-made   T. turtleneck   R. showdown

5. Unlike his pleasant brother, Nate is _____.
   C. bad-tempered   E. alma mater   A. turtleneck

6. Scott called the _____ to ask if the apartment was still available.
   I. showdown   U. seaport   A. landlord

7. The _____ young woman was always dressed in the latest fashions.
   U. custom-made   E. well-to-do   Y. turtleneck

8. At every football game, the band plays our school's _____.
   U. seaport   B. alma mater   A. showdown

9. In the old western town, the sheriff and the outlaw met for a _____.
   R. landlord   N. showdown   L. turtleneck

10. Rachel's _____ home was built exactly the way she wanted it.
    H. bad-tempered   O. landlord   R. custom-made

__ __ __ __ __ __ O __ __ __ G __ __ __ __ __ __
 8 10 6 3 9 5   1 10 6   7 2 7 6 10 4

Compound Words, II

Words from Other Languages, I

Over the centuries, English has added words from many other languages.

1. cosmonaut (n): a Russian astronaut (from Russian)

   A <u>cosmonaut</u>, Yuri Gagarin, was the first human to travel in space.

2. boulevard (n): a broad street, often lined with trees (from French)

   We walked along the <u>boulevard</u> and visited many of the small shops.

3. tortilla (n): a thin bread usually made from cornmeal (from Spanish)

   For lunch Dave had a <u>tortilla</u> with ham and cheese.

4. dinghy (n): a small boat, often carried on a larger boat (from Hindi)

   The pirates left their ship in the bay and rowed to shore in a <u>dinghy</u>.

5. maelstrom (n): a whirlpool of great size or violence; a situation that resembles a great whirlpool (from Dutch)

   Sailors warned of a <u>maelstrom</u> that destroyed ships that sailed near it.

6. wanderlust (n): a strong desire to travel (German)

   Because of <u>wanderlust</u>, Uncle Jimmy has visited dozens of countries.

7. debris (n): the scattered remains of something destroyed; ruins; rubble (from French)

   The flood left <u>debris</u> throughout the town.

8. sentinel (n): a person that stands guard; a sentry (from Italian)

   The <u>sentinel</u> stood guard at the gate of the palace.

9. flotilla (n): a small fleet of ships (from Spanish)

   The <u>flotilla</u> set sail for the New World.

10. veranda (n): a porch or balcony (usually roofed) extending around the outside of a building (from Hindi)

    We sat on the <u>veranda</u> and enjoyed the pleasant evening.

Vocabulary Tip

English continues to grow by adding new words from other languages.

34.1 Electric Eels

An electric eel is a long, eel-like fish found in northern South America. It is capable of producing a powerful electric shock that it uses for defense and to stun prey. About how much of an electric shock can the electric eel produce?

To answer the question, match each definition with its word. Choose your answers from the words after the definitions. Write the letter of each answer in the space above its definition number at the bottom of the page. You will need to divide the letters into words. Some letters are provided.

1. a person that stands guard; a sentry _____

2. a whirlpool of great size or violence; a situation that resembles a great whirlpool _____

3. a Russian astronaut _____

4. the scattered remains of something destroyed; ruins, rubble _____

5. a porch or balcony (usually roofed) extending around the outside of a building _____

6. a small fleet of ships _____

7. a broad street, often lined with trees _____

8. a small boat, often carried on a large boat _____

9. a strong desire to travel _____

10. a thin bread usually made from cornmeal _____

Answers

O. sentinel   V. wanderlust   I. cosmonaut   X. tortilla   H. veranda
U. boulevard   L. debris   D. flotilla   S. dinghy   R. maelstrom

| __ | __ | __ | __ | __ | N | __ | __ | E | __ | __ | __ | __ | T | __ |
|8|3|10|5|7|6|2|6|9|1|4|8|

34.2 The Statue of Liberty

The Statue of Liberty was given by the French people to the United States to commemorate the centennial of American independence. The statue was the work of a French sculptor. Who was he?

To answer the question, read each sentence below. Replace each under-lined word or phrase with the word that has a similar meaning. Choose your answers from the words after the sentences. Write the letter of each answer in the space above its sentence number at the bottom of the page. Some letters are provided.

1. The roofed balcony gave the house a stately appearance.

2. A sentry stood outside the captain's tent.

3. A storm wrecked the small fleet of ships.

4. Valentina Tereshkova was a Russian astronaut and the first woman in space.

5. The magician created a giant whirlpool that threatened to engulf his enemies' ships.

6. With their ship unable to come close to shore because of the shallow water, the explorers used a small boat to reach land.

7. All of her friends know of Danielle's strong desire to travel.

8. The broad, tree-lined street went through the center of the city.

9. Nick ordered cheese, lettuce, and tomatoes on a thin bread made of cornmeal for lunch.

10. After the earthquake, rescuers searched through the rubble of collapsed buildings.

Answers

D. cosmonaut   B. dinghy   R. wanderlust   L. boulevard   A. veranda
F. tortilla   O. sentinel   E. debris   I. flotilla   C. maelstrom

```
__  __  __  __  __  __  __  __      __  __  __    T   H   __  __  __  __
9   7  10   4  10   7   3   5       6   1   7            2   8   4   3
```

34.3 Freshwater

This body of water is the largest body of freshwater in the world. What is it? To answer the question, complete each sentence with the correct word. Choose your answers from the words after each sentence. Write the letter of each answer in the space above its sentence number at the bottom of the page. You will need to divide the letters into words.

1. A _____ is a thin bread made from cornmeal.
   E. flotilla   U. veranda   I. tortilla

2. Another name for a _____ is a sentry.
   A. sentinel   O. maelstrom   E. dinghy

3. _____ can inspire people to travel around the world.
   A. Veranda   U. Wanderlust   I. Debris

4. We climbed into the _____ to go to the shore.
   I. flotilla   E. maelstrom   O. dinghy

5. The _____ orbited the Earth in the Russian spacecraft.
   U. sentinel   A. wanderlust   E. cosmonaut

6. The _____ carried colonists across the Atlantic Ocean.
   S. flotilla   M. cosmonaut   A. tortilla

7. The powerful winds of the storm left _____ throughout our yard.
   R. maelstrom   P. debris   O. flotilla

8. The _____ of the house overlooked the front yard.
   K. veranda   S. boulevard   L. dinghy

9. The fight between the boys became a _____ that pulled others into the conflict.
   C. sentinel   L. maelstrom   T. wanderlust

10. The _____ was lined with trees and stately homes.
    R. boulevard   N. flotilla   A. veranda

__ __ __ __ __ __ __ __ __ __ __ __
9   2   8   5   6   3   7   5   10   1   4   10

Words from Other Languages, II

Over the centuries, English has added words from many other languages.

1. fiesta (n): a festival or religious holiday (from Spanish)

   Raul and his family had a wonderful time at the <u>fiesta</u>.

2. strudel (n): a pastry made with fruit, cheese, or nuts, rolled in a thin dough, and baked (from German)

   Apple <u>strudel</u> is Michael's favorite dessert.

3. bungalow (n): a small cottage (from Hindi)

   During our vacation we stayed in a <u>bungalow</u> at the shore.

4. hibachi (n): a portable charcoal-burning metal container with a grill (from Japanese)

   Dad grilled hamburgers and hot dogs on a <u>hibachi</u>.

5. gondola (n): a long, flat-bottomed boat; an enclosed car suspended from a cable (from Italian)

   We traveled in a <u>gondola</u> on the canals through the city of Venice.

6. coyote (n): a wolflike animal most often found in western North America (from Spanish)

   A <u>coyote</u> is an intelligent, resourceful animal.

7. typhoon (n): a hurricane occurring in the western Pacific Ocean (from Chinese)

   The <u>typhoon</u> threatened Japan.

8. attitude (n): a manner of carrying oneself; a state of mind or feeling; disposition (from Italian)

   Jeremy has a positive <u>attitude</u> about life.

9. trophy (n): something that symbolizes victory or success (from French)

   Each member of the championship wrestling team received a <u>trophy</u>.

10. brochure (n): a small pamphlet or booklet (from French)

    The travel <u>brochure</u> included a list of the island's most popular tourist attractions.

Vocabulary Tip

It has been estimated that about one in six people around the world speaks English.

35.1 Foot Size

This instrument is used in shoe stores to measure the size of a person's foot. What is it called?

To answer the question, match each definition with its word. Choose your answers from the words after the definitions. Write the letter of each answer in the space above its definition number at the bottom of the page. One letter is provided.

1. a small pamphlet or booklet _____

2. a portable charcoal-burning metal container with a grill _____

3. something that symbolizes victory or success _____

4. a festival or religious holiday _____

5. a pastry made with fruits, cheese, or nuts, rolled in a thin dough, and baked _____

6. a long, flat-bottomed boat; an enclosed car suspended from a cable _____

7. a wolflike animal most often found in western North America _____

8. a hurricane occurring in the western Pacific Ocean _____

9. a small cottage _____

10. a manner of carrying oneself; a state of mind or feeling; disposition _____

Answers

I. strudel	B. coyote	D. attitude	E. hibachi	C. gondola
N. bungalow	A. brochure	K. trophy	R. fiesta	V. typhoon

```
 __  __  __  __  __   O   __  __    __  __  __  __  __  __
 7   4   1   9   9        6   3    10   2   8   5   6   2
```

35.2 A Fictional Detective

In his story, "The Murders in the Rue Morgue," Edgar Allan Poe created the character who is considered to be the first fictional detective. What is the name of this character?

To answer the question, complete each sentence with the correct word. Choose your answers from the words after each sentence. Write the letter of each answer in the space above its sentence number at the bottom of the page. One letter is provided.

1. Serena cooked steaks on the _____ on the patio.
   M. gondola   C. trophy   S. hibachi

2. The _____ struck China with powerful winds and heavy rains.
   K. bungalow   P. typhoon   R. brochure

3. We heard the howl of a _____ last night.
   S. fiesta   N. coyote   R. gondola

4. All the townspeople looked forward to the summer _____.
   D. trophy   A. fiesta   T. hibachi

5. Jenna read the _____ that described the new health club.
   T. brochure   E. trophy   A. strudel

6. Mira has an easy-going _____ and is never upset by minor problems.
   I. attitude   E. gondola   O. typhoon

7. Callie received a _____ for being the league's batting champion.
   M. brochure   T. coyote   D. trophy

8. We rode the _____ to the top of the ski slope.
   S. attitude   E. gondola   T. trophy

9. In Kurt's opinion, his grandmother bakes the best _____ in the world.
   E. hibachi   I. fiesta   U. strudel

10. The _____ was built on the beach.
    R. gondola   L. brochure   G. bungalow

___ ___ ___ ___ ___ ___ ___   C. ___   ___ ___ ___ ___ ___
 4   9   10   9   1   5   8   7   9   2   6   3

35.3 Motion

The study of motion has a special name. What is the technical term for the study of motion?

To answer the question, read each sentence below. If the underlined word is used correctly, write the letter for correct in the space above its sentence number at the bottom of the page. If the underlined word is not used correctly, write the letter for incorrect.

1. A <u>typhoon</u> is a storm that is more powerful than a hurricane.
   L. correct   M. incorrect

2. A <u>brochure</u> is a pamphlet or booklet that provides information.
   I. correct   E. incorrect

3. A <u>coyote</u> has little resemblance to wolves or dogs.
   A. correct   I. incorrect

4. William sat on the <u>gondola</u> of the house and drank a cup of tea.
   S. correct   E. incorrect

5. Martin approaches problems with a confident <u>attitude</u>.
   S. correct   N. incorrect

6. Each year a <u>trophy</u> is awarded to the best bowler in the league.
   T. correct   W. incorrect

7. The <u>bungalow</u> was a small but comfortable home.
   K. correct   M. incorrect

8. The <u>hibachi</u> had a large built-in oven.
   U. correct   A. incorrect

9. Aunt Jan makes her <u>strudel</u> with fruits and cheese.
   C. correct   O. incorrect

10. A <u>fiesta</u> refers to a dinner at a fine restaurant.
    R. correct   N. incorrect

___   ___   ___   ___   ___   ___   ___   ___   ___   ___
 7   3   10   4   1   8   6   2   9   5

Words Based on Names

Many words are based on the names of people and places. Some words are based on mythology, especially that of the ancient Greeks and Romans.

1. tawdry (adj): gaudy, showy, or cheap in nature or appearance

   Tawdry arose from St. Audrey's lace, a type of neckpiece.

2. decibel (n): a unit that measures the intensity of sound

   Decibel comes from Alexander Graham Bell, inventor of the telephone.

3. maverick (n): an independent-minded person; an unbranded steer or horse; a steer or horse that has escaped from the herd

   Texan Samuel Maverick, who did not brand his cattle, is remembered as a maverick.

4. academy (n): a school, usually private; an association of scholars

   Academy comes from Academia, a garden where the Greek scholar Plato taught.

5. limousine (n): a large, luxurious automobile, usually driven by a chauffeur

   Limousine is named after the French region of Limousin.

6. hygiene (n): the science of health

   Hygiene is derived from Hygeia, the Greek goddess of health.

7. boycott (n): the act of refusing to use, buy, or deal with to express protest; (v): to protest by refusing to use, buy, or deal with

   Captain Charles C. Boycott, a British army office, was the first victim of a boycott.

8. odyssey (n): a long wandering journey

   After the Trojan War, Odysseus, King of Ithaca, suffered a ten-year odyssey before returning home.

9. mesmerize (v): to enthrall; to hypnotize

   Mesmerize comes from Franz Anton Mesmer, a German physician, who was also a hypnotist.

10. silhouette (n): a drawing outlining something that is filled in with a dark color

    Etienne de Silhouette, a Frenchman whose portraits were considered to be amateurish, gave us the word silhouette.

> ### Vocabulary Tip
>
> **A** word that is based on the name of a person is called an *eponym*. A word that is based on the name of a place is called a *toponym*.

36.1 The Top Three Elements

Hydrogen is the most common element in our universe. What are the next two most common elements?

To answer the question, match each definition with its word. Choose your answers from the words after the definitions. Write the letter of each answer in the space above its definition number at the bottom of the page. You will need to divide the letters into words. One letter is provided.

1. the act of refusing to use, buy, or deal with to express protest _____

2. a drawing outlining something that is filled in with a dark color _____

3. gaudy, showy, or cheap in nature or appearance _____

4. the science of health _____

5. a long, wandering journey _____

6. to enthrall; to hypnotize _____

7. a unit that measures the intensity of sound _____

8. a school, usually private; an association of scholars _____

9. a large, luxurious automobile, usually driven by a chauffeur _____

10. an independent-minded person; an unbranded steer or horse; a steer or horse that has escaped the herd _____

Answers

E. hygiene   G. mesmerize   O. tawdry   M. boycott   L. odyssey
Y. limousine   I. silhouette   H. academy   U. maverick   X. decibel

											N
8	4	5	2	10	1	3	7	9	6	4	

36.2 Used the World Over

In 1849, Walter Hunt patented this invention. What was it?

To answer the question, complete each sentence with the correct word. Choose your answers from the words after the sentences. Write the letter of each answer in the space above its sentence number at the bottom of the page. You will need to divide the letters into words. One letter is provided.

1. During his _____ the hero traveled to many lands and had many adventures.

2. The ranch hands rode out to find the _____ that had strayed from the herd.

3. The skillful speaker could _____ people with the power of his voice.

4. The _____ was the face of an old man.

5. Practicing good _____ can help keep you healthy.

6. Consumer advocates called for a _____ of the store because of its deceptive advertising.

7. Hallie has been accepted into an _____ of fine arts.

8. My sister and her boyfriend were driven to the prom in a _____.

9. Kim did not like the cheap, _____ necklace.

10. The _____ is a unit of measurement of the loudness of sound.

Answers

F. hygiene	T. limousine	I. mesmerize	P. tawdry	A. odyssey
S. academy	H. decibel	Y. boycott	E. silhouette	N. maverick

__	__	__	__	__	__	__	T	__	__	__	__
8	10	4	7	1	5	4		6	9	3	2

Words Based on Names

143

36.3 The Tall and the Short

At six feet four inches tall, Abraham Lincoln was the tallest American president. At five feet four inches tall, this president was the shortest. Who was he?

To answer the question, read each sentence below. If the underlined word is used correctly, write the letter for correct in the space above its sentence number at the bottom of the page. If the underlined word is not used correctly, write the letter for incorrect. You will need to divide the letters into words. Some letters are provided.

1. The academy offers advanced courses in mathematics and science.
   O. correct   E. incorrect

2. Hygiene is the study of different kinds of exercises.
   M. correct   S. incorrect

3. The ballerina's graceful movements could mesmerize her audience.
   M. correct   E. incorrect

4. Boycott means to discuss your ideas.
   D. correct   M. incorrect

5. Our odyssey to the mall took ten minutes.
   K. correct   I. incorrect

6. The tawdry jewels were expensive.
   R. correct   E. incorrect

7. The movie star arrived at the press conference in a big limousine.
   S. correct   U. incorrect

8. A decibel can be used to measure the speed of sound.
   A. correct   J. incorrect

9. Tess is a maverick who likes doing things her own way.
   A. correct   N. incorrect

10. Tina drew a silhouette of a young woman.
    D. correct   C. incorrect

| __ | __ | __ | __ | __ | __ | A | __ | __ | __ | __ | N |
| 8 | 9 | 4 | 6 | 2 | 3 | | 10 | 5 | 7 | 1 | |

Words for Readers and Writers

Readers and writers share a special vocabulary.

1. fictitious (adj): imaginary; fictional

   Many <u>fictitious</u> characters are modeled after real people.

2. protagonist (n): the leading character in a story

   In many stories, the <u>protagonist</u> is a hero or heroine.

3. literature (n): a body of writings in prose and verse

   Liz's mother teaches American <u>literature</u> at a college.

4. literate (adj): able to read and write; educated

   The United States has a <u>literate</u> population.

5. satire (n): a story in which the author exposes human weakness through irony, humor, or ridicule

   Gulliver's Travels by Jonathan Swift is a <u>satire</u> on human nature.

6. climax (n): the point of the greatest intensity in a story that leads to the solution of the plot

   Jared thought that the <u>climax</u> of the story was exciting.

7. manuscript (n): a typewritten or handwritten version of a book, story, article, or other work

   The author submitted his <u>manuscript</u> to his editor.

8. memoir (n): an account of the personal experiences of an author

   In her <u>memoir</u>, the author wrote of her struggle to become a writer.

9. denouement (n): the solution of the plot of a novel or play

   Riley was disappointed by the simple <u>denouement</u> of the complex novel.

10. symbolism (n): the giving of a character, object, place, or event added meaning

    <u>Symbolism</u> is a major element of many stories.

Vocabulary Tip

A dictionary is an important resource for both readers and writers.

37.1 Uncommon Presidents

Only four U.S. presidents never held any other elective office. Three of them were William H. Taft, Herbert Hoover, and Dwight D. Eisenhower. Who was the fourth?

To answer the question, match each definition with its word. Choose your answers from the words after the definitions. Write the letter of each answer in the space above its definition number at the bottom of the page.

1. an account of the personal experiences of an author _____

2. a story in which the author explains human weakness through irony, humor, or ridicule _____

3. a typewritten or handwritten version of a book, story, article, or other work _____

4. the giving of a character, object, place, or event added meaning _____

5. imaginary; fictional _____

6. able to read and write _____

7. the point of the greatest intensity in a story that leads to the solution of the plot _____

8. the solution of the plot of a novel or play _____

9. a body of writings in prose and verse _____

10. the leading character in a story _____

Answers

Y. symbolism   S. literature   G. literate   A. memoir   L. fictitious
U. denouement   E. satire   R. protagonist   T. manuscript   N. climax

| __ | __ | __ | __ | __ | __ | __ | | __. | | __ | __ | __ | __ | __ |
| 8 | 5 | 4 | 9 | 9 | 2 | 9 | | 9 | | 6 | 10 | 1 | 7 | 3 |

37.2 Driest and Lowest

This place is the driest spot in the United States and the lowest point in the Western Hemisphere. What is it?

To answer the question, complete each sentence with the correct word. Choose your answers from the words after each sentence. Write the letter of each answer in the space above its sentence number at the bottom of the page. You will need to divide the letters into words. One letter is provided.

1. The story was set in a _____ town.
   M. literature   T. fictitious   O. satire

2. The author's _____ began with his growing up on a farm.
   N. denouement   O. literature   E. memoir

3. The story was a brilliant _____ that poked fun at people's foolishness.
   E. satire   U. protagonist   A. memoir

4. Before typewriters, every _____ was handwritten.
   A. manuscript   T. symbolism   N. denouement

5. Lisa felt that the _____ of the story was a very believable character.
   M. literature   L. protagonist   W. satire

6. A democracy functions best when its people are _____.
   V. literate   R. satire   N. fictitious

7. The _____ of the story was very satisfying for Emily.
   T. literature   R. manuscript   H. denouement

8. The suspense story built to an exciting _____ with an unexpected twist.
   H. memoir   D. climax   M. protagonist

9. The author used _____ throughout the story to give objects added meaning.
   E. satire   S. denouement   L. symbolism

10. Much can be learned about a civilization through its _____.
    Y. literature   N. memoir   S. denouement

___ ___ ___ ___ ___ ___   A   ___ ___ ___ ___
 8   3   4   1   7   6   ‾   9   5   2   10

Words for Readers and Writers

147

37.3 A Lot of Mackerel

A female mackerel lays a lot of eggs. About how many eggs can this fish lay at one time?

To answer the question, read each sentence below. If the underlined word is used correctly, write the letter for correct in the space above its sentence number at the bottom of the page. If the underlined word is not used correctly, write the letter for incorrect. You will need to divide the letters into words. Some letters are provided.

1. <u>Satire</u> is an important part of the setting of every story.
   U. correct   I. incorrect

2. The <u>memoir</u> was a short story about life on Mars.
   O. correct   L. incorrect

3. An author can give an event in a story added meaning through <u>symbolism</u>.
   F. correct   H. incorrect

4. The <u>climax</u> was an interesting beginning to the story.
   D. correct   N. incorrect

5. The author used some traits of real people to create <u>fictitious</u> characters.
   A. correct   O. incorrect

6. A <u>literate</u> person can read and write.
   M. correct   H. incorrect

7. The pages of the old <u>manuscript</u> were brown and tattered.
   O. correct   N. incorrect

8. The <u>denouement</u> of a story always comes before the climax.
   E. correct   A. incorrect

9. The minor character was the <u>protagonist</u> of the story.
   U. correct   L. incorrect

10. <u>Literature</u> can be found at a library.
    I. correct   A. incorrect

__	H	__	L	__	__	__	__	__	__	__	__
5	8			3	6	1	9	2	10	7	4

Math Words

Like most subjects, mathematics has a special vocabulary.

1. approximate (adj): almost exact; close; near

   The <u>approximate</u> value of *pi* is 3.14.

2. simplify (v): to make less complex

   Nelson had to <u>simplify</u> fractions for homework.

3. constant (n): a quantity with a fixed value

   The speed of light, 299,792,458 meters per second (about 186,282 miles per second), is a <u>constant</u>.

4. calculate (v): to compute; to figure

   For math homework we had to <u>calculate</u> the circumference of a circle.

5. probability (n): a number expressing the likelihood of an event occurring; chance; possibility

   The <u>probability</u> of tossing a coin and its landing on heads is $\frac{1}{2}$.

6. formula (n): a set of symbols that expresses a mathematical statement

   Kari used a <u>formula</u> to find the area of a triangle.

7. percent (n): a part out of a hundred

   Thirty <u>percent</u> of the students in our school participate in sports.

8. midpoint (n): the point of a line segment that divides the segment into two equal parts

   Lindsay drew a line through the <u>midpoint</u> of the segment.

9. numeral (n): a symbol used to represent a number
   number 2 is a <u>numeral</u>.

10. proportion (n): a relation of equality between two ratios.

    The equation $\frac{1}{2} = \frac{2}{4}$ is a proportion.

> **Vocabulary Tip**
>
> **M**astering math vocabulary is fundamental to mastering the concepts and skills of math.

38.1 A Numbers Man

1. a relation of equality between two ratios _____
   H. proportion   E. percent   S. probability

2. a part out of a hundred _____
   A. constant   U. proportion   I. percent

3. a symbol used to represent a number _____
   I. formula   O. percent   E. numeral

4. almost exact; close; near _____
   H. proportion   R. approximate   U. constant

5. a number expressing the likelihood of an event occurring _____
   O. approximate   C. probability   R. proportion

6. a set of symbols that expresses a mathematical statement _____
   O. formula   U. numeral   M. constant

7. to make less complex _____
   A. simplify   I. calculate   S. percent

8. the point of a line segment that divides the segment into two equal parts _____
   M. proportion   P. midpoint   R. constant

9. to compute; to figure _____
   C. formula   V. approximate   M. calculate

10. a quantity with a fixed value _____
    N. percent   T. constant   W. probability

_____ _____ _____ N _____ _____ F _____ _____ _____ _____ _____ _____ _____ _____ _____ _____ S
  8   4   2   5   3   6   9   7   10   1   3   9   7   10   2   5

38.2 Hamburger

Most food historians believe that the hamburger was invented in 1900 by this man. Who was he?

To answer the question, read each sentence below. Replace the underlined word or phrase with the word that has a similar meaning. Choose your answers from the words after each sentence. Write the letter of each answer in the space above its sentence number at the bottom of the page. One letter is provided.

1. Jonah is able to <u>compute</u> a large sum of numbers in his head.
   S. percent   N. calculate   E. formula

2. Mariana tried to <u>make less complex</u> $\frac{4}{8}$.
   A. simplify   E. approximate   U. calculate

3. 42 <u>out of a 100</u> of the students bought hamburgers for lunch yesterday.
   A. proportion   H. constant   O. percent

4. In the equation $D = 45t$, t is a <u>quantity with a fixed value</u>.
   U. proportion   N. percent   E. constant

5. V is the Roman symbol used to <u>represent the number</u> that equals 5.
   S. numeral   K. constant   R. formula

6. $\frac{3}{4} = \frac{6}{8}$ is an example of a <u>relation of equality between two ratios</u>.
   N. probability   T. percent   S. proportion

7. Every line segment has a <u>point that divides the segment into two equal parts</u>.
   E. formula   U. midpoint   W. constant

8. The <u>chance</u> of rolling a 13 with two standard dice is 0.
   J. percent   L. probability   C. proportion

9. $P = 4s$ is the <u>set of symbols</u> that can be used to find the perimeter of a square.
   L. formula   T. percent   N. midpoint

10. The <u>almost exact</u> length of the room is 20 feet.
    E. midpoint   A. constant   I. approximate

__ __ __ __ __   __ __ S̲ __ __ __
8   3   7 10   5   9   2   6   4   1

Math Words

38.3 Roller Coaster

Most historians agree that the first roller coaster in the United States opened in New York City in 1884. Exactly where in the city was this roller coaster built?

   To answer the question, complete each sentence with the correct word. Choose your answers from the words after the sentences. Write the letter of each answer in the space above its sentence number at the bottom of the page. You will need to divide the letters into words.

1. The _____ for finding the area of a rectangle is $A = l \times w$.

2. A _____ shows that two ratios are equal.

3. Six out of one hundred is 6 _____.

4. A number whose value does not change is a _____.

5. After adding two fractions, you should _____ your answer.

6. The _____ divided the segment into two smaller segments of 5 inches each.

7. A synonym for *number* is _____.

8. The _____ of randomly picking the number 21 out of a jar with 100 different numbers is small.

9. The _____ weight of our dog is 85 pounds.

10. Sara used a pencil and paper to _____ the answer to the multiplication problem.

Answers

I. constant	C. probability	L. calculate	O. percent	S. formula
A. numeral	E. proportion	Y. midpoint	N. approximate	D. simplify

___ ___ ___ ___ ___ ___ ___ ___ ___ ___ ___
8   3   9   2   6   4   1   10   7   9   5

Math Words

Social Studies Words

Social studies is a course of study that focuses on the relationships between people and countries.

1. aristocracy (n): a hereditary privileged ruling class

   During the country's civil war, the <u>aristocracy</u> was overthrown.

2. despot (n): a ruler with absolute power

   The <u>despot</u> used his power to oppress his people.

3. alliance (n): a formal pact of union; agreement; accord

   Several countries formed an <u>alliance</u> for mutual defense.

4. diplomat (n): a person skilled in conducting international relations

   A successful <u>diplomat</u> has great skills for dealing with people.

5. import (n): a product brought into a country for trade or sale; (v): to bring a product into a country for trade or sale

   Oil is a major <u>import</u> of the United States.

   Countries around the world <u>import</u> products from the United States.

6. legislation (n): the act or procedures of enacting laws; lawmaking

   The primary responsibility of the U.S. Congress is <u>legislation</u>.

7. circumnavigate (v): to sail completely around

   Ferdinand Magellan and his crew set out to <u>circumnavigate</u> the world.

8. currency (n): any form of money in actual use; money

   The <u>currency</u> of the United States is based on the dollar.

9. capitalism (n): an economic system in which businesses are privately owned and operated for profit

   <u>Capitalism</u> is the economic system of the United States.

10. export (n): a product sent to another country for trade or sale; (v): to send a product to another country for trade or sale

    Oil is an important <u>export</u> of countries in the Middle East.

    Many countries <u>export</u> cars to the United States.

Vocabulary Tip

Social studies often includes geography, history, and government.

39.1 Your Muscles

The main job of your muscles is to make body movements possible. What is the study of muscles and their relation to human movement called?

To answer the question, match each definition with its word. Choose your answers from the words after each definition. Write the letter of each answer in the space above its definition number at the bottom of the page. One letter is provided.

1. to sail completely around _____
   U. alliance   E. export   I. circumnavigate

2. a person skilled in conducting international relations _____
   I. diplomat   A. aristocracy   O. despot

3. an economic system in which businesses are privately owned and operated for profit _____
   A. currency   I. aristocracy   E. capitalism

4. a product brought into a country for trade or sale _____
   S. capitalism   Y. import   N. export

5. a ruler with absolute power _____
   I. aristocracy   O. despot   U. diplomat

6. a product sent to another country for trade or sale _____
   W. currency   N. export   R. import

7. a formal pact of union; agreement; accord _____
   E. aristocracy   A. capitalism   O. alliance

8. the act or procedures of enacting laws; lawmaking _____
   K. legislation   T. alliance   M. aristocracy

9. a hereditary privileged ruling class _____
   M. alliance   G. aristocracy   W. despot

10. any form of money in actual use; money _____
    L. currency   S. legislation   U. capitalism

__	__	__	__	S	__	__	__	__	__	__
8	1	6	3	2	7	10	5	9	4	

39.2 A Legendary Basketball Player

This man was the first player in the National Basketball Association to score 38,000 points. Who was he?

To answer the question, match each word on the left with the key words of its definition on the right. Write the letter of each answer in the space above the word's number at the bottom of the page.

Words

1. alliance _____

2. legislation _____

3. capitalism _____

4. export _____

5. import _____

6. circumnavigate _____

7. currency _____

8. diplomat _____

9. aristocracy _____

10. despot _____

Keys Words of Definitions

D. to sail completely around

A. a product brought into a country for trade or sale

E. a ruler with absolute power

L. money

K. a hereditary privileged ruling class

U. a formal pact of union

B. a person skilled in international relations

R. an economic system with private ownership of business

J. a product sent to another country for trade or sale

M. procedures of enacting laws

__ __ __ __ __ __   __ __ __ __ __ - __ __ __ __ __ __
9 5 3 10 10 2   5 8 6 1 7   4 5 8 8 5 3

39.3 A Presidential Resignation

This man was the only U.S. president to resign from office. Who was he?

To answer the question, complete each sentence with the correct word. Choose your answers from the words after each sentence. Write the letter of each answer in the space above its sentence number at the bottom of the page. You will need to divide the letters into words. Some letters are provided.

1. _____ is an economic system characterized by private ownership.
   S. Legislation   R. Capitalism   U. Aristocracy

2. For someone to _____ the world, he or she must sail around it completely.
   E. despot   U. diplomat   O. circumnavigate

3. Countries that _____ products send those products to other countries.
   S. circumnavigate   N. export   T. import

4. Countries that _____ products allow other countries to send products to them.
   A. alliance   H. export   I. import

5. Members of the _____ enjoyed many privileges during the Middle Ages.
   H. aristocracy   M. alliance   E. capitalism

6. Lawmakers worked long into the night trying to pass the _____.
   E. alliance   I. legislation   O. currency

7. The U.S. _____ met with leaders of France.
   T. legislation   D. diplomat   N. aristocracy

8. _____ is the form of money a country uses.
   S. Alliance   M. Legislation   X. Currency

9. A _____ is a ruler who wields complete power.
   R. despot   T. diplomat   J. capitalism

10. Various citizens' groups formed an _____ to discourage drunk driving.
    C. alliance   O. aristocracy   M. import

__	__	__	__	A	__	__	__	__	__	__	N
9	4	10	5		1	7	3	6	8	2	

Social Studies Words

Science Words

Science is knowledge acquired from observation, experimentation, and analysis, and then organized in a system.

1. germinate (v): to begin or cause to grow

    Many plants <u>germinate</u> in the spring.

2. antibiotic (n): a substance that destroys or slows the growth of bacteria

    Penicillin is an <u>antibiotic.</u>

3. extinct (adj): no longer existing or living; inactive

    Dinosaurs have been <u>extinct</u> for about 65 million years.

4. biology (n): the science of living things and life processes

    Lyle's brother is studying <u>biology</u> in high school.

5. decomposition (n): the process of the decay of dead plants and animals

    <u>Decomposition</u> returns vital nutrients to the environment.

6. organism (n): a living plant or animal

    A frog is an <u>organism,</u> and so is a tree.

7. terrestrial (adj): of or pertaining to the Earth or its inhabitants; living or growing on land

    Jason was certain that the creature he saw was not <u>terrestrial.</u>

8. ecosystem (n): a community of plants and animals and their environment

    A pond is an example of an <u>ecosystem.</u>

9. photosynthesis (n): the process by which green plants use sunlight to convert water and carbon dioxide into food

    <u>Photosynthesis</u> is not possible without light.

10. energy (n): power or vigor in action; the capacity for vigorous action

    Scientists define <u>energy</u> as the ability to do work.

Vocabulary Tip

The word *science* comes from the Latin word *scire,* which means "to know."

40.1 Moon Rocks

During the Apollo expeditions to the moon, U.S. astronauts collected and brought moon rocks back to Earth for study. About how much rock did they bring back?

To answer the question, match each definition with its word. Choose your answers from the words after the definitions. Write the letter of each answer in the space above its definition number at the bottom of the page. You will need to divide the letters into words. Some letters are provided.

1. of or pertaining to the Earth or its inhabitants _____

2. to begin or cause to grow _____

3. the process of decay of dead plants and animals _____

4. power or vigor in action; the capacity for vigorous action _____

5. a substance that destroys or slows the growth of bacteria _____

6. a living plant or animal _____

7. no longer existing or living; inactive _____

8. the process by which green plants use sunlight to convert water and carbon dioxide into food _____

9. a community that includes plants and animals and their environment _____

10. the science of living things and life processes _____

Answers

U. energy   E. terrestrial   N. photosynthesis   O. germinate   T. ecosystem
G. biology   P. organism   H. decomposition   D. extinct   I. antibiotic

__	__	__	__	__	__	__	__	__	R	__	__	__	__	__	__	__	S
1	5	10	3	9	3	4	8	7		1	7	6	2	4	8	7	

40.2 Mount Rushmore

Mount Rushmore is a memorial known for its carved portraits of George Washington, Thomas Jefferson, Abraham Lincoln, and Theodore Roosevelt. It is located in South Dakota and was completed in 1941. Who was the sculptor that directed the work?

To answer the question, match each word on the left with the key words of its definition on the right. Write the letter of each answer in the space above the word's number at the bottom of the page.

Words	Key Words of Definitions
1. organism _____	N. power or vigor in action
2. energy _____	L. the process by which green plants make food
3. germinate _____	B. of or pertaining to the Earth
4. decomposition _____	R. no longer existing or living
5. photosynthesis _____	Z. a living plant or animal
6. terrestrial _____	U. a substance that kills or slows the growth of bacteria
7. antibiotic _____	G. a community of plants and animals
8. extinct _____	M. to begin or cause to grow
9. ecosystem _____	O. the science of living things
10. biology _____	T. the decay of dead plants and animals

— — — — — —   — — — — — — —
9 7 4 1 10 2   6 10 8 9 5 7 3

40.3 Twinkies

People around the world enjoy Hostess Twinkies, which were invented in 1930. Who invented them?

To answer the question, read each sentence below. If the underlined word is used correctly, write the letter for correct in the space above its sentence number at the bottom of the page. If the underlined word is not used correctly, write the letter for incorrect.

1. An <u>organism</u> is any living or nonliving thing in the environment.
   U. correct   E. incorrect

2. Plants make food through the process of <u>photosynthesis</u>.
   E. correct   I. incorrect

3. We use various forms of <u>energy</u> to provide the power for our machines.
   R. correct   N. incorrect

4. An <u>extinct</u> volcano has been inactive for a long time.
   A. correct   O. incorrect

5. When a plant dies, it is about to <u>germinate</u>.
   U. correct   A. incorrect

6. <u>Decomposition</u> describes the process of how plants begin to grow.
   S. correct   D. incorrect

7. Human beings are examples of <u>terrestrial</u> creatures.
   S. correct   R. incorrect

8. The plants, animals, and soil of a forest are parts of an <u>ecosystem</u>.
   J. correct   P. incorrect

9. Doctors should never prescribe an <u>antibiotic</u> for an illness caused by bacteria.
   M. correct   W. incorrect

10. <u>Biology</u> is the study of living and nonliving things.
    T. correct   M. incorrect

___ ___ ___ ___ ___   ___ ___ ___ ___ ___
 8   4   10   2   7   6   1   9   5   3

Word List

Following are the vocabulary words and the lesson in which they appear:

abolish, L. 4
abrupt, L. 12
absence, L. 19
abstain, L. 26
absurd, L. 2
academy, L. 36
accelerate, L. 27
access, L. 11
accommodate, L. 24
acquaintance, L. 23
adequate, L. 1
adversary, L. 20
adverse, L. 10
advocate, L. 13
aerial, L. 15
aftereffect, L. 16
agenda, L. 23
allegiance, L. 4
alliance, L. 39
allusion, L. 9
alma mater, L. 33
altitude, L. 13
amateur, L. 22
ambitious, L. 18
amiable, L. 30
amnesty, L. 19

ample, L. 31
amplify, L. 24
anecdote, L. 11
annoyance, L. 18
anonymous, L. 15
anthropologist, L. 22
antibiotic, L. 40
antidote, L. 11
apparent, L. 3
apparition, L. 22
appease, L. 26
applicant, L. 22
appraise, L. 10
apprise, L. 10
approximate, L. 38
aristocracy, L. 39
arrogant, L. 28
artifact, L. 22
ascent, L. 8
assent, L. 8
assert, L. 26
asteroid, L. 14
astronomy, L. 14
attendance, L. 8
attendants, L. 8
attitude, L. 35

available, L. 30
averse, L. 10
aviary, L. 21
bad-tempered, L. 33
banquet, L. 20
bazaar, L. 7
belittle, L. 17
belligerent, L. 28
besiege, L. 17
bestow, L. 25
biology, L. 40
bizarre, L. 7
blockade, L. 19
bluff, L. 5
boisterous, L. 31
borough, L. 7
boulevard, L. 34
bountiful, L. 2
boycott, L. 36
braggart, L. 23
brochure, L. 35
brokenhearted, L. 33
bungalow, L. 35
burro, L. 7
burrow, L. 7
calamitous, L. 30

calculate, L. 38
capacious, L. 30
capital, L. 8
capitalism, L. 39
capitol, L. 8
Capitol, L. 8
capitulate, L. 24
casual, L. 3
catastrophe, L. 20
celestial, L. 31
chauffeur, L. 22
chronicle, L. 14
chronological, L. 14
circumnavigate, L. 39
cite, L. 8
clarity, L. 21
click, L. 10
climax, L. 37
clique, L. 10
collaborate, L. 25
comply, L. 25
confidant, L. 10
confident, L. 10
conscience, L. 9
conscious, L. 9
conserve, L. 24
console, L. 6
constant, L. 38
contagious, L. 9
contemplate, L. 24
contiguous, L. 9
continual, L. 9
continuous, L. 9
contribute, L. 12
controversial, L. 29
controversy, L. 23
conventional, L. 28
cosmonaut, L. 34
council, L. 7
counsel, L. 7
coyote, L. 35
cringe, L. 2
culminate, L. 27
currency, L. 39
curtail, L. 4

customary, L. 4
custom-made, L. 33
cymbal, L. 8
cynical, L. 31
debris, L. 34
decibel, L. 36
decomposition, L. 40
deference, L. 10
democracy, L. 15
demography, L. 15
denouement, L. 37
designate, L. 27
despondent, L. 30
despot, L. 39
determine, L. 24
dexterous, L. 31
difference, L. 10
diminish, L. 25
dinghy, L. 34
diplomat, L. 39
disburse, L. 11
discomfit, L. 11
discomfort, L. 11
discreet, L. 8
discrete, L. 8
disinterested, L. 10
disperse, L. 11
distort, L. 25
doctrine, L. 12
document, L. 12
downpour, L. 32
drawbridge, L. 32
dynasty, L. 20
ecosystem, L. 40
eerie, L. 28
efficient, L. 3
elicit, L. 11
eligible, L. 11
elusive, L. 11
emerge, L. 10
eminent, L. 10
empathy, L. 15
emphasize, L. 2
encompass, L. 24
energy, L. 40

engulf, L. 27
enigma, L. 23
entrepreneur, L. 22
epidemic, L. 15
eradicate, L. 25
erasable, L. 10
erupt, L. 12
evidence, L. 23
excess, L. 11
exclusive, L. 28
exorbitant, L. 28
expand, L. 9
expend, L. 9
expertise, L. 20
export, L. 39
extinct, L. 40
extravagant, L. 3
facade, L. 22
facetious, L. 3
fallible, L. 30
far-fetched, L. 32
fiasco, L. 20
fickle, L. 1
fictitious, L. 37
fiesta, L. 35
flamboyant, L. 1
flotilla, L. 34
flounder, L. 5
fluent, L. 31
foreword, L. 7
formidable, L. 3
formula, L. 38
forward, L. 7
fraudulent, L. 19
frostbite, L. 32
generate, L. 14
genial, L. 31
germinate, L. 40
gondola, L. 35
gorilla, L. 8
guerilla, L. 8
gullible, L. 3
hamper, L. 6
hibachi, L. 35
hospitable, L. 13

hospital, L. 13
hover, L. 27
humility, L. 1
husky, L. 6
hygiene, L. 36
illegible, L. 11
illicit, L. 11
illiterate, L. 17
illogical, L. 17
illusion, L. 9
illusive, L. 11
immerge, L. 10
imminent, L. 10
impassable, L. 16
imply, L. 11
import, L. 39
improper, L. 16
inaudible, L. 16
incense, L. 5
incite, L. 7
inconspicuous, L. 2
inconvenient, L. 30
incredible, L. 10
incredulous, L. 10
indecision, L. 16
indigent, L. 11
indignant, L. 11
indisputable, L. 28
infer, L. 11
infirmary, L. 18
infuriate, L. 27
ingenious, L. 9
ingenuous, L. 9
ingredient, L. 21
inhabitant, L. 22
insight, L. 7
insignia, L. 13
inspect, L. 13
instance, L. 8
instants, L. 8
intensive, L. 29
interact, L. 16
international, L. 16
interpreter, L. 21
interstellar, L. 16

invalid, L. 6
invaluable, L. 29
invincible, L. 2
irascible, L. 10
irregular, L. 17
irresistible, L. 17
irresponsible, L. 17
judicious, L. 28
kindred, L. 22
laboratory, L. 18
landlord, L. 33
launch, L. 6
leased, L. 7
least, L. 7
legacy, L. 21
legislation, L. 39
lichen, L. 8
lightheaded, L. 32
liken, L. 8
limousine, L. 36
literate, L. 37
literature, L. 37
loathe, L. 1
lobbyist, L. 21
logical, L. 3
lubricate, L. 27
lumber, L. 6
maelstrom, L. 34
makeshift, L. 32
malfunction, L. 17
manuscript, L. 37
maroon, L. 6
maverick, L. 36
mechanic, L. 14
mechanism, L. 14
memoir, L. 37
memorandum, L. 20
mesmerize, L. 36
midpoint, L. 38
mutual, L. 30
necessity, L. 19
negotiate, L. 25
nervous, L. 18
notable, L. 3
notorious, L. 31

novice, L. 2
numeral, L. 38
nutritious, L. 18
object, L. 5
obliterate, L. 26
odyssey, L. 36
old-fashioned, L. 33
opponent, L. 1
organism, L. 40
orthodontist, L. 15
orthodox, L. 15
outcome, L. 32
outlandish, L. 3
overbearing, L. 16
overdue, L. 16
paternal, L. 12
patience, L. 8
patients, L. 8
patriarch, L. 12
percent, L. 38
perception, L. 20
perjury, L. 23
perpetrate, L. 9
perpetuate, L. 9
persevere, L. 27
personal, L. 9
personnel, L. 9
philosopher, L. 14
photosynthesis, L. 40
plague, L. 21
plait, L. 7
plate, L. 7
plausible, L. 31
plumage, L. 21
poach, L. 5
posterity, L. 21
potential, L. 28
precede, L. 9
precise, L. 4
predominant, L. 29
premonition, L. 23
prescribe, L. 24
prevail, L. 24
prior, L. 2
probability, L. 38

proceed, L. 9
profit, L. 7
progeny, L. 14
prophet, L. 7
proportion, L. 38
proprietor, L. 20
protagonist, L. 37
prudent, L. 29
pseudonym, L. 15
pulverize, L. 27
racket, L. 6
random, L. 31
ratify, L. 24
ravenous, L. 29
recede, L. 17
recommend, L. 25
reel, L. 6
refrain, L. 5
refurbish, L. 17
refuse, L. 26
refute, L. 26
reinforce, L. 25
relevant, L. 4
reluctant, L. 4
renowned, L. 30
replenish, L. 25
reputable, L. 4
resistance, L. 18
respect, L. 13
respectably, L. 11
respectfully, L. 11
respectively, L. 11
rifle, L. 5
rush hour, L. 32
sagacious, L. 4
sage, L. 21

satire, L. 37
saunter, L. 27
seaport, L. 33
sensible, L. 2
sentinel, L. 34
serene, L. 1
shingles, L. 5
showdown, L. 33
sight, L. 8
significant, L. 13
silhouette, L. 36
simplify, L. 38
site, L. 8
sluggish, L. 29
sophisticated, L. 14
spectacle, L. 13
stalemate, L. 23
staple, L. 5
stationary, L. 7
stationery, L. 7
stern, L. 6
stoop, L. 5
straight, L. 7
strait, L. 7
strenuous, L. 28
strudel, L. 35
substantial, L. 4
suppress, L. 26
symbol, L. 8
symbolism, L. 37
sympathy, L. 15
tawdry, L. 36
tedious, L. 29
tenet, L. 23
terrestrial, L. 40
terrify, L. 19

torrid, L. 1
tortilla, L. 34
treason, L. 20
tributary, L. 12
trivial, L. 29
trophy, L. 35
turbulent, L. 19
turtleneck, L. 33
typhoon, L. 35
ultimate, L. 30
unify, L. 26
uninterested, L. 10
unity, L. 19
urban, L. 18
vanquish, L. 26
variety, L. 12
various, L. 12
veracious, L. 9
veranda, L. 34
verify, L. 26
versatile, L. 1
veteran, L. 18
vicious, L. 1
vigilant, L. 2
vilify, L. 19
violence, L. 19
vital, L. 29
vocal, L. 13
voracious, L. 9
wanderlust, L. 34
waterfront, L. 32
well-to-do, L. 33
whirlwind, L. 32
wondrous, L. 1

Answer Key

Lesson 1

1.1 1. T 2. G 3. O 4. E 5. H 6. U 7. Y 8. M 9. S 10. I
Mighty Mouse

1.2 1. P 2. A 3. S 4. E 5. E 6. E 7. A 8. C 9. H 10. Y
Chesapeake Bay

1.3 1. L 2. O 3. A 4. D 5. T 6. N 7. S 8. H 9. M 10. E
The Headless Horseman

Lesson 2

2.1 1. R 2. A 3. A 4. L 5. G 6. I 7. S 8. L 9. N 10. F
Niagara Falls

2.2 1. L 2. R 3. Y 4. Y 5. H 6. A. 7. P 8. S 9. L 10. U
Sally Murphy

2.3 1. U 2. I 3. O 4. G 5. N 6. F 7. S 8. D 9. T 10. A
St. Augustine, Florida

Lesson 3

3.1 1. U 2. E 3. C 4. S 5. H 6. M 7. N 8. B 9. J 10. A
James Buchanan

3.2 1. U 2. T 3. W 4. O 5. H 6. S 7. C 8. P 9. A 10. D
Ah, what's up, Doc?

3.3 1. S 2. A 3. L 4. T 5. I 6. M 7. C 8. B 9. N 10. U
Uncle Tom's Cabin

Lesson 4

4.1 1. S 2. E 3. T 4. E 5. S. 6. A 7. R 8. T 9. T 10. R
Tess Trueheart

4.2 1. H 2. A 3. M 4. T 5. P 6. W 7. O 8. E 9. D 10. F
two fathoms deep

4.3 1. O 2. I 3. M 4. R 5. C 6. H 7. B 8. N 9. A 10. L
Abraham Lincoln

Lesson 5

5.1 1. S 2. O 3. A 4. W 5. R 6. N 7. G 8. E 9. T 10. H
The Greatest Show on Earth

5.2 1. E 2. A 3. N 4. I 5. H 6. R 7. C 8. D 9. O 10. S
icosahedron

5.3 1. P 2. S 3. G 4. F 5. W 6. A 7. U 8. L 9. O 10. R
a group of owls

Lesson 6

6.1 1. O 2. N 3. R 4. E 5. A 6. M 7. L 8. D 9. P 10. I
palindrome

6.2 1. N 2. Y 3. P 4. H 5. R 6. T 7. O 8. E 9. S 10. M
sphygmomanometer

6.3 1. Y 2. P 3. M 4. C 5. G 6. H 7. A 8. O 9. E 10. R
Grace Murray Hopper

Lesson 7

7.1 1. R 2. E 3. C 4. N 5. O 6. V 7. A 8. L 9. I 10. D
Leonardo Da Vinci

7.2 1. O 2. O 3. I 4. D 5. E 6. E 7. H 8. T 9. T 10. L
theodolite

7.3 1. I 2. R 3. O 4. A 5. E 6. N 7. W 8. T 9. F 10. L
float in water

Lesson 8

8.1 1. A 2. O 3. U 4. R 5. L 6. P 7. S 8. M 9. E 10. T
Samuel Prescott

8.2 1. O 2. T 3. E 4. H 5. R 6. A 7. E 8. B 9. T 10. M
bathometer

8.3 1. I 2. E 3. O 4. S 5. N 6. D 7. D 8. R 9. L 10. S
Old Ironsides

Lesson 9

9.1 1. R 2. O 3. C 4. D 5. N 6. O 7. D 8. N 9. S 10. Y
Sandra Day O'Connor

9.2 1. I 2. T 3. Y 4. E 5. I 6. E 7. N 8. N 9. N 10. N
ninety-nine

9.3 1. N 2. E 3. E 4. H 5. I 6. T 7. T 8. F 9. T 10. O
The Flintstones

Lesson 10

10.1 1. A 2. O 3. S 4. T 5. T 6. S 7. A 8. N 9. H 10. M
Thomas Nast

10.2 1. T 2. A 3. E 4. U 5. O 6. R 7. G 8. C 9. S 10. H
Oscar the Grouch

10.3 1. A 2. O 3. N 4. C 5. V 6. D 7. R 8. L 9. G 10. E
Grover Cleveland

Lesson 11

11.1 1. E 2. A 3. I 4. M 5. E 6. F 7. R 8. F 9. G 10. A
male giraffe

11.2 1. N 2. T 3. H 4. L 5. A 6. U 7. T 8. S 9. E 10. U
The *Nautilus*

11.3 1. I 2. A 3. I 4. A 5. T 6. T 7. W 8. L 9. F 10. L
William Taft

Lesson 12

12.1 1. O 2. C 3. R 4. A 5. P 6. E 7. T 8. B 9. I 10. L
elliptical orbit

12.2 1. A 2. K 3. N 4. A 5. T 6. M 7. H 8. E 9. U 10. T
Tutankhamen

12.3 1. O 2. A 3. T 4. S 5. I 6. O 7. E 8. N 9. R 10. D
rotates on its side

Lesson 13

13.1 1. G 2. O 3. N 4. K 5. D 6. B 7. I 8. M 9. R 10. C
mockingbird

13.2 1. A 2. O 3. L 4. N 5. E 6. W 7. H 8. C 9. R 10. B
Charlie Brown

13.3 1. R 2. S 3. M 4. N 5. I 6. R 7. B 8. T 9. L 10. E
Tim Berners-Lee

Lesson 14

14.1 1. N 2. A 3. E 4. Z 5. D 6. R 7. H 8. S 9. O 10. U
horrendous hazardous

14.2 1. H 2. M 3. S 4. T 5. B 6. N 7. E 8. W 9. A 10. L
a name with one syllable

14.3 1. A 2. E 3. N 4. I 5. M 6. G 7. F 8. O 9. D 10. R
Roman god of fire

Lesson 15

15.1 1. L 2. T 3. M 4. N 5. E 6. E 7. T 8. E 9. S 10. T
settlement

15.2 1. L 2. H 3. U 4. S 5. C 6. F 7. A 8. D 9. B 10. O
Bashful and Doc

15.3 1. E 2. M 3. O 4. L 5. L 6. M 7. N 8. C 9. A 10. M
cloned mammal

Lesson 16

16.1 1. R 2. S 3. I 4. O 5. G 6. A 7. T 8. M 9. H 10. W
Martha Washington

16.2 1. N 2. I 3. T 4. Y 5. L 6. M 7. S 8. B 9. W 10. F
swim but not fly

16.3 1. E 2. I 3. N 4. B 5. H 6. O 7. C 8. L 9. R 10. V
olive branch

Lesson 17

17.1 1. M 2. R 3. T 4. Q 5. A 6. U 7. O 8. I 9. L 10. E
liquid at room temperature

17.2 1. L 2. L 3. D 4. T 5. O 6. Y 7. N 8. T 9. L 10. B
Lyle and Talbot

17.3 1. A 2. A 3. A 4. N 5. L 6. I 7. H 8. M 9. W 10. I
Mauna Loa, Hawaii

Lesson 18

18.1 1. P 2. Y 3. R 4. W 5. C 6. O 7. T 8. M 9. E 10. H
The Newport Mercury

18.2 1. I 2. N 3. B 4. E 5. O 6. R 7. U 8. B 9. L 10. B
blue ribbon

18.3 1. K 2. C 3. L 4. O 5. E 6. A 7. S 8. T 9. I 10. B
Oswald the Lucky Rabbit

Lesson 19

19.1 1. I 2. Y 3. E 4. R 5. K 6. G 7. N 8. F 9. J 10. O
Ken Griffey, Junior and Senior

19.2 1. E 2. E 3. R 4. V 5. R 6. R 7. O 8. H 9. H 10. B
Herbert Hoover

19.3 1. S 2. D 3. C 4. R 5. A 6. P 7. E 8. O 9. L 10. G
a good spot or place

Lesson 20

20.1 1. N 2. R 3. M 4. A 5. S 6. O 7. J 8. F 9. C 10. E
James Fenimore Cooper

20.2 1. E 2. A 3. Y 4. H 5. R 6. H 7. T 8. E 9. B 10. S
bathysphere

20.3 1. L 2. O 3. S 4. Y 5. R 6. G 7. E 8. V 9. B 10. N
bears live young

Lesson 21

21.1 1. A 2. P 3. T 4. Y 5. R 6. I 7. P 8. B 9. H 10. B
Happy Rabbit

21.2 1. D 2. L 3. J 4. N 5. S 6. C 7. O 8. G 9. I 10. A
Sailor Jack and Bingo

21.3 1. U 2. H 3. J 4. I 5. R 6. A 7. Q 8. E 9. C 10. N
Jacqueline Cochran

Lesson 22

22.1 1. D 2. S 3. A 4. E 5. Y 6. R 7. K 8. I 9. T 10. W
sky-tinted water

22.2 1. T 2. M 3. E 4. E 5. H 6. S 7. T 8. R 9. A 10. P
The Empire State (Building)

22.3 1. E 2. E 3. A 4. A 5. B 6. H 7. U 8. L 9. W 10. L
a blue whale

Lesson 23

23.1 1. E 2. T 3. O 4. Y 5. F 6. I 7. S 8. M 9. P 10. R
Professor Moriarty

23.2 1. K 2. A 3. L 4. I 5. S 6. H 7. C 8. R 9. T 10. E
thicket-clearers

23.3 1. U 2. A 3. I 4. A 5. A 6. N 7. U 8. R 9. M 10. Q
an aquarium

Lesson 24

24.1 1. C 2. R 3. T 4. S 5. A 6. H 7. E 8. B 9. K 10. N
the Snickers Bar

24.2 1. N 2. S 3. I 4. H 5. R 6. P 7. O 8. D 9. C 10. Y
hydroponics

24.3 1. T 2. H 3. A 4. R 5. H 6. I 7. O 8. A 9. P 10. A
Porthos, Athos, Aramis

Lesson 25

25.1 1. G 2. S 3. E 4. A 5. I 6. O 7. B 8. R 9. L 10. N
one billion grains

25.2 1. O 2. R 3. N 4. O 5. E 6. F 7. C 8. C 9. N 10. T
confectioner

25.3 1. A 2. H 3. T 4. P 5. E 6. N 7. O 8. R 9. I 10. S
Princess of Ethiopia

Lesson 26

26.1 1. E 2. A 3. R 4. O 5. S 6. H 7. F 8. J 9. T 10. M
Thomas Jefferson

26.2 1. I 2. A 3. O 4. E 5. M 6. N 7. L 8. A 9. S 10. M
Amelia Simmons

26.3 1. A 2. N 3. E 4. X 5. L 6. J 7. O 8. P 9. K 10. M
James Knox Polk

Lesson 27

27.1 1. A 2. A 3. D 4. N 5. O 6. J 7. L 8. E 9. G 10. L
Jane Goodall

27.2 1. I 2. E 3. T 4. E 5. R 6. R 7. G 8. R 9. V 10. A
great river

27.3 1: S 2. O 3. M 4. Y 5. R 6. I 7. C 8. L 9. H 10. E
Shirley Chisholm

Lesson 28

28.1 1. S 2. H 3. F 4. U 5. N 6. D 7. T 8. O 9. E 10. R
Ernest Rutherford

28.2 1. P 2. A 3. E 4. S 5. H 6. L 7. T 8. D 9. I 10. N
the Spice Island

28.3 1. I 2. O 3. P 4. T 5. E 6. C 7. R 8. L 9. A 10. N
International Coastal Cleanup

Lesson 29

29.1 1. K 2. M 3. U 4. E 5. R 6. A 7. T 8. Y 9. H 10. O
to make room for your heart

29.2 1. E 2. O 3. T 4. L 5. I 6. L 7. S 8. S 9. G 10. O
speleologist

29.3 1. D 2. S 3. A 4. E 5. E 6. C 7. S 8. U 9. U 10. O
succedaneous (teeth)

Lesson 30

30.1 1. R 2. U 3. A 4. H 5. S 6. T 7. D 8. O 9. E 10. N
one hundred thousand

30.2 1. P 2. B 3. I 4. I 5. E 6. B 7. H 8. L 9. I 10. L
bibliophile

30.3 1. S 2. A 3. A 4. U 5. M 6. Y 7. C 8. D 9. I 10. S
Damascus, Syria

Lesson 31

31.1 1. Y 2. H 3. U 4. S 5. T 6. A 7. I 8. O 9. N 10. X
sixty thousand

31.2 1. T 2. A 3. R 4. P 5. R 6. O 7. Y 8. C 9. M 10. G
cryptogram

31.3 1. I 2. I 3. T 4. L 5. S 6. A 7. C 8. B 9. S 10. L
ballistics

Lesson 32

32.1 1. B 2. Y 3. A 4. W 5. L 6. K 7. I 8. E 9. D 10. S
Disney spelled backward

32.2 1. Y 2. O 3. E 4. R 5. H 6. X 7. J 8. I 9. D 10. N
John Kennedy, Richard Nixon

32.3 1. E 2. V 3. C 4. O 5. A 6. U 7. T 8. F 9. S 10. N
close to five thousand

Lesson 33

33.1 1. A 2. N 3. E 4. I 5. T 6. V 7. M 8. D 9. S 10. O
Simon, Theodore, Dave

33.2 1. N 2. F 3. Y 4. O 5. A 6. Q 7. E 8. I 9. S 10. T
Sea of Tranquility

33.3 1. U 2. H 3. I 4. T 5. C 6. A 7. E 8. B 9. N 10. R
brain, courage, heart

Lesson 34

34.1 1. O 2. R 3. I 4. L 5. H 6. D 7. U 8. S 9. V 10. X
six hundred volts

34.2 1. A 2. O 3. I 4. D 5. C 6. B 7. R 8. L 9. F 10. E
Frederic Bartholdi

34.3 1. I 2. A 3. U 4. O 5. E 6. S 7. P 8. K 9. L 10. R
Lake Superior

Lesson 35

35.1 1. A 2. E 3. K 4. R 5. I 6. C 7. B 8. V 9. N 10. D
Brannock Device

35.2 1. S 2. P 3. N 4. A 5. T 6. I 7. D 8. E 9. U 10. G
Auguste C. Dupin

35.3 1. M 2. I 3. I 4. E 5. S 6. T 7. K 8. A 9. C 10. N
kinematics

Lesson 36

36.1 1. M 2. I 3. O 4. E 5. L 6. G 7. X 8. H 9. Y 10. U
helium, oxygen

36.2 1. A 2. N 3. I 4. E 5. F 6. Y 7. S 8. T 9. P 10. H
the safety pin

36.3 1. O 2. S 3. M 4. M 5. I 6. E 7. S 8. J 9. A 10. D
James Madison

Lesson 37

37.1 1. A 2. E 3. T 4. Y 5. L 6. G 7. N 8. U 9. S 10. R
Ulysses S. Grant

37.2 1. T 2. E 3. E 4. A 5. L 6. V 7. H 8. D 9. L 10. Y
Death Valley

37.3 1. I 2. L 3. F 4. N 5. A 6. M 7. O 8. A 9. L 10. I
a half million

Lesson 38

38.1 1. H 2. I 3. E 4. R 5. C 6. O 7. A 8. P 9. M 10. T
Prince of Mathematics

38.2 1. N 2. A 3. O 4. E 5. S 6. S 7. U 8. L 9. L 10. I
Louis Lassen

38.3 1. S 2. E 3. O 4. I 5. D 6. Y 7. A 8. C 9. N 10. L
Coney Island

Lesson 39

39.1 1. I 2. I 3. E 4. Y 5. O 6. N 7. O 8. K 9. G 10. L
kinesiology

39.2 1. U 2. M 3. R 4. J 5. A 6. D 7. L 8. B 9. K 10. E
Kareem Abdul-Jabbar

39.3 1. R 2. O 3. N 4. I 5. H 6. I 7. D 8. X 9. R 10. C
Richard Nixon

Lesson 40

40.1 1. E 2. O 3. H 4. U 5. I 6. P 7. D 8. N 9. T 10. G
eight hundred pounds

40.2 1. Z 2. N 3. M 4. T 5. L 6. B 7. U 8. R 9. G 10. O
Gutzon Borglum

40.3 1. E 2. E 3. R 4. A 5. A 6. D 7. S 8. J 9. W 10. M
James Dewar

Made in the USA
Middletown, DE
29 June 2018